PRENTICE-HALL FOUNDATIONS OF PHILOSOPHY SERIES

Virgil Aldrich	Philosophy of Art
William Alston	Philosophy of Language
Stephen Barker	Philosophy of Mathematics
Roderick Chisholm	Theory of Knowledge
William Dray	Philosophy of History
Joel Feinberg	Social Philosophy
William Frankena	Ethics
Carl Hempel	Philosophy of Natural Science
John Hick	Philosophy of Religion
David Hull	Philosophy of Biological Science
Willard Van Orman Quine	Philosophy of Logic
Richard Rudner	Philosophy of Social Science
Wesley Salmon	Logic
Jerome Shaffer	Philosophy of Mind
Richard Taylor	Metaphysics

Elizabeth and Monroe Beardsley, editors

second edition

PHILOSOPHY
OF RELIGION

John Hick

UNIVERSITY OF BIRMINGHAM, ENGLAND

PRENTICE-HALL, INC.
Englewood Cliffs, New Jersey

Library of Congress Cataloging in Publication Data

Hick, John.
 Philosophy of religion.

 (Foundations of philosophy series)
 Bibliography: p.
 1. Religion—Philosophy. I. Title.
BL51.H494 1973   200'.1   72-5429
ISBN 0-13-663948-8

For Eleanor, Mark, Peter, and Michael

in the hope
that this little book may assist in their education

© *1973 , 1963 by*
PRENTICE-HALL, INC.
Englewood Cliffs, New Jersey

10 9 8 7 6 5

PRENTICE-HALL INTERNATIONAL, INC., London
PRENTICE-HALL OF AUSTRALIA, PTY. LTD., Sydney
PRENTICE-HALL OF CANADA, LTD., Toronto
PRENTICE-HALL OF INDIA PRIVATE LIMITED, New Delhi
PRENTICE-HALL OF JAPAN, INC., Tokyo

FOUNDATIONS OF PHILOSOPHY

Many of the problems of philosophy are of such broad relevance to human concerns, and so complex in their ramifications, that they are, in one form or another, perennially present. Though in the course of time they yield in part to philosophical inquiry, they may need to be rethought by each age in the light of its broader scientific knowledge and deepened ethical and religious experience. Better solutions are found by more refined and rigorous methods. Thus, one who approaches the study of philosophy in the hope of understanding the best of what it affords will look for both fundamental issues and contemporary achievements.

Written by a group of distinguished philosophers, the Foundations of Philosophy Series aims to exhibit some of the main problems in the various fields of philosophy as they stand at the present stage of philosophical history.

While certain fields are likely to be represented in most introductory courses in philosophy, college classes differ widely in emphasis, in method of instruction, and in rate of progress. Every instructor needs freedom to change his course as his own philosophical interests, the size and makeup of his classes, and the needs of his students vary from year to year. The nineteen volumes in the Foundations of Philosophy Series—each complete in itself, but complementing the others—offer a new flexibility to the instructor, who can create his own textbook by combining several volumes as he wishes, and can choose different combinations at different times. Those volumes that are not used in an introductory course will be found valuable, along with other texts or collections of readings, for the more specialized upper-level courses.

Elizabeth Beardsley / *Monroe Beardsley*

CONTENTS

Contents

9

Introduction

WHAT IS THE PHILOSOPHY OF RELIGION?

What is the philosophy of religion? Until recently it was generally understood to mean religious philosophizing in the sense of the philosophical defense of religious convictions. It was seen as continuing the work of "natural," distinguished from "revealed," theology.[1] Its program was to demonstrate rationally the existence of God, thus preparing the way for the claims of revelation. But it seems better to call this endeavor "natural theology," and to term the wider philosophical defense of religious beliefs "apologetics." Then we may reserve the name "philosophy of religion" for what (by analogy with philosophy of science, philosophy of art, etc.) is its proper meaning, namely, *philosophical thinking about religion.*

Philosophy of religion, then, is not an organ of religious teaching. Indeed, it need not be undertaken from a religious standpoint at all. The atheist, the agnostic, and the man of faith all can and do philosophize about religion. Philosophy of religion is, accordingly, not a branch of theology (meaning by "theology" the systematic formulation of religious beliefs), but a branch

[1] These terms are defined on p. 53.

of philosophy. It studies the concepts and propositions of theology and the reasonings of theologians, as well as the prior phenomena of religious experience and the activities of worship upon which theology ultimately rests and out of which it has arisen.

Philosophy of religion is thus a second-order activity, standing at one remove from its subject matter. It is not itself a part of the religious realm but is related to it as the philosophy of law is related to the realm of legal phenomena and to juridical concepts and reasonings, or the philosophy of art to artistic phenomena and to the categories and methods of aesthetic discussion. The philosophy of religion is thus related to the particular religions and theologies of the world as the philosophy of science relates to the special sciences. It seeks to analyze concepts such as God, holy, salvation, worship, creation, sacrifice, eternal life, etc., and to determine the nature of religious utterances in comparison with those of everyday life, scientific discovery, morality, and the imaginative expressions of the arts.

This understanding of the scope of the philosophy of religion excludes material that is sometimes included. Most notably, it excludes philosophy of life and philosophy of existence. The latter, under the name of "existentialism," is an important factor on the contemporary cultural scene.[2] It includes a variety of elements. Existential thinking is thinking that is desperately serious and passionately concerned. A philosopher is thinking existentially when, instead of being a detached and uncaring spectator, he is personally involved in the problem with which he is dealing, his entire being engaged in the philosophical struggle. In this sense, all the greatest western philosophers from Plato to Wittgenstein have thought existentially.

Most of the writings which identify themselves as "existentialist" are concerned with the description of human existence as it is immediately experienced. They stress its temporal character and make central use of themes such as anxiety, finitude, guilt, despair, dread of death and of "non-being," doubt, meaninglessness, loneliness, and self-estrangement. The language of existentialism tends to be the language of the soul's distress. It depicts twentieth-century urban life in the industrialized West as the spiritual nightmare that it can be for minds acutely sensitive to the decay of tradition, the collapse of established cultural forms, and the threat of a nuclear holocaust. Existentialist literature—which includes drama, poetry, novels, autobiography, and psychological description and analysis, as well as formal and systematic discussions—expresses the neuroses of an age that finds itself being carried into the unknown on the wheel of immense and bewildering changes.

Although the artistic expression and the psychological description of the disintegrative aspects of contemporary life are not part of the philosophy

[2] For an introduction to existentialism see, e.g., William Barrett, *Irrational Man* (Garden City, N.Y.: Doubleday & Company, Inc., Anchor Books, 1962).

of religion as it is understood in this book, the combination of existentialism with systematic reflection in such a thinker as Paul Tillich does provide important material for discussion, and several aspects of Tillich's thought are accordingly studied at various points in these chapters.

A complete treatise on the philosophy of religion would have to investigate the nature of religion in general and would deal with all the main ideas of the many different religions. It is not possible in this short book to undertake either of these tasks. The nature of religion is a vast and complex subject that can be approached from a bewildering variety of viewpoints. Religion is one thing to the anthropologist, another to the sociologist, another to the psychologist (and another again to the next psychologist!), another to the Marxist, another to the mystic, another to the Zen Buddhist, and yet another to the Jew or the Christian. As a result, there are a great variety of anthropological, sociological, psychological, naturalistic, and religious theories of the nature of religion. There is, consequently, no universally accepted definition of religion and quite possibly there never will be. For our present purpose, however, this does not matter. Since, in a book of this length, we have no space to discuss religion in general or the immense range of religious phenomena, we must very largely restrict attention to a single stream of religious life and thought. We shall accordingly be considering the philosophical questions provoked by the religious ideas that lie behind our western Atlantic civilization and that still form the main religious options within our culture. These are the ideas of Christianity and Judaism, centering upon their concept of God. But it is also important to see how contemporary philosophical methods can be applied to the ideas of quite different religious traditions; and this will be done, as a sample, in relation to the Indian belief in reincarnation (Chapter 8). It is also necessary, in the "one world" of today, to face the problem of the apparently conflicting truth claims of the various religions of the world. This issue, which constitutes one of the main growing points of the philosophy of religion today, will be explored in the final chapter.

CHAPTER ONE

The Judaic-Christian Concept of God

MONOTHEISM   The terms used for the main ways of thinking about God are formed around either the Greek word for God, *theos,* or its Latin equivalent, *deus.*

Beginning at the negative end of the scale, *atheism* (not-Godism) is the belief that there is no God of any kind; and *agnosticism,* which means literally "not-know-ism," is in this context the belief that we do not have sufficient reason either to affirm or to deny God's existence. *Scepticism* simply means doubting. *Naturalism* is the theory that every aspect of human experience, including man's moral and religious life, can be adequately described and accounted for in terms of his existence as a gregarious and intelligent animal whose life is organic to his material environment.

Moving to the positive side of the scale, *deism* can refer either to the idea of an "absentee" god who long ago set the universe in motion and has thereafter left it alone or, as an historical term, to the position of the eighteenth-century English deists, who taught that natural theology[1] alone is religiously sufficient. *Theism* (often used as a synonym for monotheism)

---

[1] For a definition of "natural theology," see p. 53.

is strictly belief in a deity, but is generally used to mean belief in a personal deity. *Polytheism* (many-gods-ism) is the belief, common among primitive peoples and reaching its classic expression in ancient Greece and Rome, that there are a multitude of personal gods, each holding sway over a different department of life.[2] A person whose religion is a form of *Henotheism* believes that there are many gods but restricts his allegiance to one of them, generally the god of his own tribe or people. *Pantheism* (God-is-all-ism) is the belief, perhaps most impressively expounded by some of the poets, that God is identical with nature or with the world as a whole. *Monotheism* (one-God-ism) is the belief that there is but one supreme Being, who is personal and moral and who seeks a total and unqualified response from his human creatures. This idea first came to fully effective consciousness among men in the words, "Hear, O Israel: The Lord our God is one Lord; and you shall love the Lord your God with all your heart, and with all your soul, and with all your might."[3] As these historic words indicate, the Hebraic understanding of God, continued in Christianity, is emphatically monotheistic.

The Old Testament (which constitutes the sacred writings of Judaism and part, along with the New Testament, of the sacred writings of Christianity) documents the rise of monotheism in constant but never fully resolved struggle with polytheism and henotheism. The God of the Hebrews was originally worshiped as a tribal god, Jahweh of Israel, over against such foreign deities as Dagon of the Philistines and Chemosh of the Moabites. But the insistent, though at first incredible, message of the great prophets of the eighth, seventh, and sixth centuries before Christ (above all, Amos, Hosea, first Isaiah, Jeremiah, and second Isaiah) was that Jahweh was not only the God of the Hebrews but the Maker of heaven and earth and the Judge of all history and of all peoples.[4] The Hebrew prophets taught that although God had indeed summoned their own nation to a special mission as the living medium of his revelation to the world, he was not only their God but also Lord of the gentiles or foreigners. A great biblical scholar says, "Hebrew monotheism arose through the intuitive perception that a God who is righteous first and last must be as uni-

---

[2] For example, in the Greek pantheon, Poseidon (god of the sea), Ares (god of war), and Aphrodite (goddess of love).

[3] Deut. 6:4–5. Earlier than this, in the fourteenth century B.C., the Egyptian pharaoh Ikhnaton had established the sole worship of the sun god, Aton; but immediately after Ikhnaton's death this early monotheism was overcome by the prevailing national polytheism. NOTE: All biblical quotations, except where otherwise noted, are reprinted by permission and are taken from the Revised Standard Version of the Holy Bible (New York: Thomas Nelson & Sons). Copyright 1946, 1952 by the Division of Christian Education of the National Council of Churches.

[4] From the book *Essays and Addresses on the Philosophy of Religion* (Vol. I) by Baron Von Hugel. Published by E. P. Dutton & Co., Inc. and used with the permission of E. P. Dutton & Co., Inc. and J. M. Dent & Sons Ltd.

versal as righteousness itself."[5] His service must involve a responsibility not only to fellow members of the same "household of faith" but to all one's fellow creatures of every race and group.

It is a corollary of the prophets' teaching concerning the lordship of God over all human life that there is no special religious sphere set apart from the secular world but that the whole sweep of man's existence stands in relation to God. Thus religion is secularized, or—putting it the other way about—ordinary life takes on a religious meaning. In some words of H. Richard Niebuhr:

> The counterpart of this secularization, however, is the sanctification of all things. Now every day is the day that the Lord has made; every nation is a holy people called by him into existence in its place and time and to his glory; every person is sacred, made in his image and likeness; every living thing, on earth, in the heavens, and in the waters is his creation and points in its existence toward him; the whole earth is filled with his glory; the infinity of space is his temple where all creation is summoned to silence before him.[6]

The difficulty involved in maintaining such a faith in practice, even within a culture that has been permeated for centuries by monotheistic teaching, is evidenced by the polytheistic and henotheistic elements in our own life. A religiously sensitive visitor from another planet would doubtless report that we divide our energies in the service of many deities—the god of money, of a business corporation, of success, of power, the status gods, and (for a brief period once a week) the God of Judaic-Christian faith. When we rise above this practical polytheism, it is generally into a henotheistic devotion to the nation, or to the American way of life, in order to enjoy our solidarity with an in-group against the out-groups. In this combination of elements there is no continuity with the pure monotheism of the prophets and of the New Testament, with its vivid awareness of God as the Lord of history whose gracious purpose embracing all life renders needless the frantic struggle to amass wealth, power, and prestige at the expense of others.

INFINITE,   This monotheistic faith, finding its primary expres-
SELF-EXISTENT   sions in the commands and prayers, psalms and
                      prophecies, parables and teachings of the Bible, has
been philosophically elaborated and defined through the long history of Christian thought; and because Christianity has become a more theologically articulated religion than Judaism, most of our material will be taken from this source.

[5] C. H. Dodd, *The Authority of the Bible,* 1929 (New York: Harper & Row, Publishers, Torchbooks, 1958), p. 111.

[6] H. Richard Niebuhr, *Radical Monotheism and Western Culture* (New York: Harper & Row, Publishers, 1960), pp. 52–53.

A basic idea which recurs at innumerable points is that God is infinite or unlimited.

It is this insistence that God is unlimited being that led Paul Tillich to hold that we should not say even that God *exists,* since this would be a limiting statement about him. "Thus the question of the existence of God can be neither asked nor answered. If asked, it is a question about that which by its very nature is above existence, and therefore the answer— whether negative or affirmative—implicitly denies the nature of God. It is as atheistic to affirm the existence of God as it is to deny it. God is being-itself, not *a* being."[7] This paradox, as it must sound in the mouth of a theologian, that "God does not exist" is, however, not as startling as it may at first appear. It operates as a vivid repudiation of every form of belief in a finite deity. Tillich means, not that the term "God" does not refer to any reality, but that the reality to which it refers is not merely one among others, not even the first or the highest, but rather the very source and ground of all being. Tillich is, in effect, urging a restriction of the term "exists" to the finite and created realm, thereby rendering it improper to ask of the infinite creator whether he exists, or to affirm or deny his existence. But it is only on the basis of this restricted usage that Tillich repudiates the statement that God exists. He is emphasizing the point, which was familiar to the medieval scholastics, that the creator and the created cannot be said to exist in precisely the same sense.

God then, according to Judaism and Christianity, is or has unlimited being; and the various divine "attributes" or characteristics are so many ways in which the infinite divine reality *is,* or exists, or has being.

First among these attributes we may place what the scholastics called *aseity* (from the Latin *a se esse,* being from oneself), usually translated as "self-existence." The concept of self-existence, as it occurs in the work of the great theologians, contains two elements.

1. God is not dependent either for his existence or for his characteristics upon any reality other than himself. He has not been created by any higher being. There is nothing outside him capable either of constituting or of destroying him. He just *is,* and is what he is, in infinite richness and plenitude of being as the ultimate, unconditioned, all-conditioning reality. In abstract terms, God has absolute ontological independence.

2. It follows from this that God is eternal, without beginning or end. If he had a beginning, there would have to be a prior reality to bring him into being; and in order for his existence to be terminated, there would have to be some reality capable of effecting this. Each of these ideas is excluded by his absolute ontological independence.

7 Paul Tillich, *Systematic Theology* I (Welwyn, Hertfordshire: James Nisbet & Company Ltd. and Chicago: University of Chicago Press, 1951), p. 237. Copyright 1951 by the University of Chicago.

The eternity of God means more, however, than simply that he exists without beginning or end, as is indicated in this passage from Anselm (1033–1109):

Indeed You exist neither yesterday nor today nor tomorrow but are absolutely outside all time. For yesterday and today and tomorrow are completely in time; however, You, though nothing can be without You, are nevertheless not in place or time but all things are in You. For nothing contains You, but You contain all things.[8]

CREATOR   God is conceived in the Judaic-Christian tradition as the infinite, self-existent Creator of everything that exists, other than himself. In this doctrine, creation means far more than fashioning new forms from an already given material (as a builder makes a house, or a sculptor a statue); it means creation out of nothing—*creatio ex nihilo*—the summoning of a universe into existence when otherwise there was only God. There are two important corollaries of this idea.

First, it entails an absolute distinction between God and his creation, such that it is logically impossible for a creature to become the Creator. That which has been created will forever remain the created. To all eternity the Creator is the Creator and the creature is creature. Any thought of man becoming God is thus ruled out as meaningless by the Judaic-Christian conception of creation.

A second corollary is that the created realm is absolutely dependent upon God as its Maker and as the source of its continued existence. Hence we find that this radical notion of creation *ex nihilo* expresses itself in prayer and liturgy as a sense of dependence upon God for man's being from moment to moment. We have a part in the universe not by some natural right, but by the grace of God; and each day is a gift to be received in thankfulness and responsibility toward the divine Giver.

What are the scientific implications of this idea? Does it entail that the creation of the physical universe took place at some specific moment in the far distant past?

Thomas Aquinas (1224/5–1274) held that the idea of creation does not necessarily rule out the possibility that the created universe may be eternal. It is, he thought, conceivable that God has been creative from all eternity, so that although his universe has a created and dependent status, it is nevertheless without a beginning. He also held, however, that although the concept of creation does not in itself imply a beginning, Christian revelation asserts a beginning; and on this ground he rejected the idea of an

---

[8] *Proslogion,* Chap. 19, tr. M. J. Charlesworth, *St. Anselm's Proslogion* (Oxford: Clarendon Press, 1965), pp. 141–43.

eternal creation.[9] A different and perhaps more fruitful approach is suggested by Augustine's thought that the creation did not take place *in time* but that time is itself an aspect of the created world.[10] If this is true, it may also be, as relativity theory suggests, that space-time is internally infinite—that is to say, from within the space-time continuum the universe is found to be unbounded both spatially and temporally. In that case it has no initial state. But it may nevertheless, although internally infinite, depend for its existence and its nature upon the will of a transcendent God. And this is the essence of the religious doctrine of creation: namely, that the universe as a spatiotemporal whole exists in virtue of its relation to God. Such a doctrine is neutral as between the various rival theories of the origin of the present state of the universe developed in scientific cosmology.[11]

Needless to say, the magnificent creation story in the first two chapters of the Book of Genesis is not regarded as a piece of scientific description by responsible religious thinkers today. It is seen rather as the classic mythological expression of the faith that the whole natural order is a divine creation. Indeed, this way of reading religious myths is very ancient, as the following passage, written by Origen in the third century, indicates.

For who that has understanding will suppose that the first, and second, and third day, and the evening and the morning, existed without a sun, and moon, and stars? and that the first day was, as it were, also without a sky? And who is so foolish as to suppose that God, after the manner of a husbandman, planted a paradise in Eden, towards the east, and placed in it a tree of life, visible and palpable, so that one tasting of the fruit by the bodily teeth obtained life? and again, that one was a partaker of good and evil by masticating what was taken from the tree? And if God is said to walk in the paradise in the evening, and Adam to hide himself under a tree, I do not suppose that any one doubts that these things figuratively indicate certain mysteries....[12]

PERSONAL   The conviction that God is personal, *He* rather than *It*, has always been plainly implied both in the biblical writings and in later Jewish and Christian devotional and theological literature. In the Old Testament God speaks in personal terms (for example, "I am the God of your father, the God of Abraham, the God of Isaac, and

---

[9] *Summa Theologica,* Part I, Question 46, Art. 2. There is a good discussion of Aquinas's doctrine of creation in F. C. Copleston, *Aquinas* (Harmondsworth, Middlesex: Penguin Books Ltd., 1955), pp. 136f.

[10] *Confessions,* Book 11, Chap. 13; *City of God,* Book 11, Chap. 6.

[11] Some of the current theories about the origin of the universe are discussed in Ian Barbour, *Issues in Science and Religion* (Englewood Cliffs, N.J.: Prentice-Hall, Inc., 1966).

[12] *De Principiis,* IV, I, 16. *The Writings of the Ante-Nicene Fathers,* IV, 365.

the God of Jacob")[13] and the prophets and psalmists address him in personal terms (for example, "Hear my cry, O God, listen to my prayer.").[14] In the New Testament the same conviction as to the personal character of God is embodied in the figure of fatherhood that was constantly used by Jesus as the most adequate earthly image with which to think of God.

Although belief in the Thou-hood of God thus pervades the Judaic-Christian tradition, the explicit doctrine that God is personal is of comparatively recent date, being characteristic of the theology of the nineteenth and especially of the twentieth century. In our own time the Jewish religious thinker Martin Buber has pointed to the two radically different kinds of relationship, I–Thou and I–It;[15] and a number of Christian theologians have developed the implications of the insight that God is the divine Thou who has created us as persons in his own image and who always deals with us in ways which respect our personal freedom and responsibility.[16] (This theme will be taken up again in the discussion of revelation and faith in Chapter 5.)

Most theologians speak of God as "personal" rather than as "a Person." The latter phrase suggests the picture of a magnified human individual. (Thinking of the divine in this way is called anthropomorphism, from the Greek *anthropos,* man, and *morphe,* shape—"in the shape of man.") The statement that God is personal is accordingly intended to signify that God is "at least personal," that whatever God may be beyond our conceiving, he is not less than personal, not a mere It in relation to man, but always the higher and transcendent Thou.

By implication, this belief raises the question of the analogical or symbolic character of human speech about God, which will be discussed further in Chapter 6.

LOVING, GOOD   Goodness and love are generally treated as two further attributes of God. But in the New Testament God's goodness, love, and grace are all virtually synonymous, and the most characteristic of the three terms is love.

13 Exod. 3:6.
14 Psalms 61:1.
15 *I and Thou,* 1923, trans. 2nd ed. (New York: Charles Scribner's Sons, 1958).
16 Among them, John Oman, *Grace and Personality,* 1917 (London: Fontana Library, 1960 and New York: Association Press, 1961); Emil Brunner, *God and Man* (London: Student Christian Movement Press Ltd., 1936) and *The Divine–Human Encounter* (Philadelphia: The Westminster Press, 1942 and London: Student Christian Movement Press Ltd., 1944); H. H. Farmer, *The World and God* (Welwyn, Hertfordshire: James Nisbet & Company Ltd., 1935) and *God and Men* (Welwyn, Hertfordshire: James Nisbet & Company Ltd., 1948 and Nashville, Tenn.: Abingdon Press, 1961).

In order to understand what the New Testament means by the love of God it is necessary first to distinguish the two kinds of love signified by the Greek words *eros* and *agape*. *Eros* is "desiring love," love which is evoked by the desirable qualities of the beloved. This love is evoked by and depends upon the lovableness of its objects. He loves her because she is pretty, charming, cute. She loves him because he is handsome, manly, clever. Parents love their children because they are *their* children. However, when the New Testament speaks of God's love for mankind it employs a different term, *agape*. This word already existed in the Greek language but was not generally used to convey any special meaning distinct from *eros* until New Testament writers, through their use of the word, imprinted upon it the meaning of "giving love." Unlike *eros, agape* is unconditional and universal in its range. It is given to someone, not because he has special characteristics, but simply because he *is,* because he is there as a person. The nature of *agape* is to value a person in such wise as actively to seek his or her deepest welfare and fulfillment. It is in this sense that the New Testament speaks of God's love for mankind. When it is said, for example, that "God is Love"[17] or that "God so loved the world...,"[18] the word used is *agape* and its cognates.

God's universal love for his human creatures, a love not rooted in their virtue or desert but in God's own nature as *agape*, is the basis for that side of religion which knows God as the final succor and security of man's life: "God is our refuge and strength, a very present help in trouble."[19] The ultimate of grace is believed to be also the ultimate of power, the sovereign love which guarantees man's final fulfillment and well-being.

The infinite divine love also gives rise to that side of religious experience in which God is known as claiming the total obedience of a man's life. God is thought of as "Lord" and "King" as well as "Father." The divine commands come with the accent of absolute and unconditional claim, a claim which may not be set in the balance with any other interest whatever, not even life itself. This element of demand can be viewed as an expression of the divine love, seeking the best that lies potentially within man. Even between human beings there is nothing so inexorably demanding as a love that seeks our highest good and cannot be content that we be less than our potential best. Because it is infinite, the love of the Creator for the creatures made in his image implies a moral demand of this kind that is absolute and unqualified.

In this exposition we have subsumed the goodness of God under the love of God. But this idea does not avoid an important philosophical prob-

17 I John 4:8.
18 John 3:16.
19 Psalms 46:1.

lem concerning the belief that God is good. Does this belief imply a moral standard external to God, in relation to which he can be said to be good? Or alternatively, does it mean that God is good by definition? Is the Creator offered as the final standard of goodness, so that his nature, whatever it may be, is the norm of goodness?

Either position involves difficulties. If God is good in relation to some independent standard by which he may be judged, he is no longer the sole ultimate reality. He exists in a moral universe whose character is not of his own making. If, however, God is good by definition, and it is a tautology that whatever he commands is right, certain other implications arise which are hard to accept. Suppose that beginning tomorrow, God wills that human beings should do all the things which he has formerly willed they should not do. Now hatred, cruelty, selfishness, envy, and malice are virtues. God commands them; and since God is good, whatever he wills is right. This possibility is entailed by the view we are considering; yet it conflicts with the assumption that our present moral principles and intuitions are generally sound, or at least that they do not point us in a completely wrong direction.

Perhaps the most promising resolution of the dilemma is a frankly circular one. Good is a relational concept, referring to the fulfillment of a being's nature and basic desires. When humans call God good, they mean that his existence and activity constitute the condition of man's highest good. The presupposition of such a belief is that God has made human nature in such a way that his highest good is to be found in relation to God. Ethics and value theory in general are independent of religion in that their principles can be formulated without any mention of God; yet they ultimately rest upon the character of God, who has endowed man with the nature whose fulfillment defines his good.

In connection with the goodness of God, reference should also be made to the divine "wrath," which has played so prominent a part in pharisaic and puritanical thought. "Flee from the wrath to come" has been the warning burden of much religious preaching. Much of this preaching has, ironically, embraced the very anthropomorphism which Saint Paul, whose writings supply the standard texts concerning the Wrath of God, so carefully avoided. C. H. Dodd, in his study of Saint Paul, pointed out that Paul never describes God as being wrathful, but always speaks of the Wrath of God in a curiously impersonal way to refer to the inevitable reaction of the divinely appointed moral order of the Universe upon wrongdoing. The conditions of human life are such that for an individual or a group to infringe upon the structure of the personal order is to court disaster. "This disaster Paul calls, in traditional language, 'The Wrath,' or much more rarely, 'The Wrath of God.'...'The Wrath,' then, is revealed before our eyes as the increasing horror of sin working out its hideous law of cause and effect."[20]

HOLY   Taken separately, each of these characteristics of
God, as he is conceived in the Judaic-Christian tradi-
tion, presents itself as an abstract philosophical idea. But the religious person, conscious of standing in the unseen presence of God, is overwhelmingly aware of the divine reality as infinitely other and greater than he. This sense of the immensity and otherness of God was expressed with unforgettable vividness by Isaiah:

> *To whom then will you liken God,*
> *or what likeness compare with him?*
> *The idol! a workman casts it,*
> *and a goldsmith overlays it with gold*
> *and casts for it silver chains.*
> *He who is improverished chooses for an offering*
> *wood that will not rot;*
> *he seeks out a skillful craftsman*
> *to set up an image that will not move.*
> *Have you not known? Have you not heard?*
> *Has it not been told you from the beginning?*
> *Have you not understood from the foundations of the earth?*
> *It is he who sits above the circle of the earth,*
> *and its inhabitants are like grasshoppers;*
> *who stretches out the heavens like a curtain,*
> *and spread them like a tent to dwell in;*
> *who brings princes to nought,*
> *and makes the rulers of the earth as nothing...*
> *To whom then will you compare me,*
> *that I should be like him? says the Holy One.*
> *Lift up your eyes on high and see:*
> *who created these?*[21]

Again, God is "...the high and lofty One who inhabits eternity, whose name is Holy,"[22] whose "...thoughts are not your thoughts, neither are your ways my ways, says the Lord. For as the heavens are higher than the

---

[20] C. H. Dodd, *The Meaning of Paul for Today,* 1920 (New York: World Publishing Company, Meridian Books, 1957), pp. 63–64.

[21] Isa. 40:18–23, 25–26.

[22] Isa. 57:15.

earth, so are my ways higher than your ways and my thoughts than your thoughts."[23] The awareness of God as holy is the awareness of One who is terrifyingly mysterious, an intensity of being in relation to which men are virtually nothing, a perfection in whose eyes "...all our righteousnesses are as filthy rags,"[24] a purpose and power before which we human beings can only bow down in silent awe.

We may now sum up the Judaic-Christian concept of God: God is conceived as the infinite, eternal, uncreated, personal reality, who has created all that exists other than himself, and who has revealed himself to his human creatures as holy and loving.

---

[23] Isa. 55:8–9.
[24] Isa. 64:6 (King James Version).

CHAPTER TWO

Grounds for Belief in God

The conception of God outlined in the preceding chapter is the outcome of many centuries of development during which some of the most acute minds of the western world have sought, in a cooperative venture, to discover the fuller meaning and deeper implications of the stream of religious experience recorded in the Bible. Throughout the remainder of this book, as we raise philosophical questions about the Judaic-Christian concept of God, our central and controlling question must be concerned with the reasons behind the belief that there is any such Being. We must examine the grounds on which religious persons have claimed to know that God exists.

In this chapter we shall examine the most important of the philosophical arguments offered to justify belief in the reality of God. These traditional "theistic proofs" are of great philosophical interest and have been receiving more rather than less attention from both secular and religious writers in recent years.

THE ONTOLOGICAL   The ontological argument for the existence of God
ARGUMENT   was first developed by Anselm, one of the Christian
                        Church's most original thinkers and the greatest theo-
logian ever to have been archbishop of Canterbury.[1]

Anselm begins by concentrating the Christian concept of God into the
formula: *"a being than which nothing greater can be conceived."* It is
clear that by "greater" Anselm means more perfect, rather than spatially
bigger.[2] It is important to notice that the idea of the most perfect conceivable being is different from the idea of the most perfect being that there is.
The ontological argument could not be founded upon this latter notion,
for although it is true by definition that the most perfect being that there
is exists, there is no guarantee that this being is what Anselm means by
God. Consequently, instead of describing God as the most perfect being
that there is, Anselm describes God as the being who is so perfect that no
more perfect can even be conceived.

FIRST FORM OF THE ARGUMENT

In the next and crucial stage of his argument Anselm distinguishes between something, *x,* existing in the mind only and its existing in reality
as well. If the most perfect conceivable being existed only in the mind,
we should then have the contradiction that it is possible to conceive of a
yet more perfect being, namely, the same being existing in reality as well
as in the mind. Therefore, the most perfect conceivable being must exist in
reality, as well as in the mind. Anselm's own formulation of this classic
piece of philosophical reasoning is found in the second chapter of the
Proslogion.

If then that-than-which-a-greater-cannot-be-thought exists in the mind alone, this
same that-than-which-a-greater-*cannot*-be-thought is that-than-which-a-greater-*can*-
be-thought. But this is obviously impossible. Therefore there is absolutely no
doubt that something-than-which-a-greater-cannot-be-thought exists both in the
mind and in reality.

SECOND FORM OF THE ARGUMENT

In his third chapter Anselm states the argument again, directing it
now not merely to God's existence but to his uniquely *necessary* existence.
God is defined in such a way that it is impossible to conceive of him not

---

[1] The ontological argument is to be found in Chaps. 2–4 of Anselm's *Proslogion.*
Among the best English translations are those by M. J. Charlesworth in *St. Anselm's
Proslogion* (Oxford: Clarendon Press, 1965)—from which the quotations in this
chapter are taken—and Arthur C. McGill in *The Many-Faced Argument,* eds. J. H.
Hick and A. C. McGill (New York: The Macmillan Company, 1967, and London:
Macmillan & Company Ltd., 1968).

[2] On occasions (for example, *Proslogion,* Chaps. 14 and 18) Anselm uses "better"
(*melius*) in place of "greater."

existing. The core of this notion of necessary being is self-existence (*aseity*).[3] Since God in his infinite perfection is not limited in or by time, the twin possibilities of his having ever come to exist and of his ever ceasing to exist are alike excluded, and his nonexistence is rendered impossible. The argument now runs as follows.

For something can be thought to exist that cannot be thought not to exist. Hence, if that-than-which-a-greater-cannot-be-thought can be thought not to exist, then that-than-which-a-greater-cannot-be-thought is not the same as that-than-which-a-greater-cannot-be-thought, which is absurd. Something-than-which-a-greater-cannot-be-thought exists so truly then, that it cannot be even thought not to exist.

CRITICISMS OF THE ARGUMENT

In introducing the ontological argument Anselm refers to the psalm-ist's "fool" who says in his heart, "There is no God."[4] Even such a person, he says, possesses the idea of God as the greatest conceivable being; and when we unpack the implications of this idea we see that such a being must actually exist. The first important critic of the argument, Gaunilon, a monk at Marmoutiers in France and a contemporary of Anselm's, accordingly entitled his reply *In Behalf of the Fool*. He claims that Anselm's reasoning would lead to absurd conclusions if applied in other fields, and he sets up a parallel ontological argument for the most perfect island. Gaunilon spoke of the most perfect of islands rather than (as he should have done) of the most perfect conceivable island; but his argument could be rephrased in terms of the latter idea. Given the idea of such an island, by using Anselm's principle we can argue that unless it exists in reality it cannot be the most perfect conceivable island!

Anselm's reply, emphasizing the uniqueness of the idea of God to show that the ontological reasoning applies only to it, is based upon his second form of the argument. The element in the idea of God which is lacking in the notion of the most perfect island is *necessary* existence. An island (or any other material object) is by definition a part of the contingent world. The most perfect island, so long as it is genuinely an island—"a piece of land surrounded by water" and thus part of the physical globe—is by definition a dependent reality, which can without contradiction be thought not to exist, and therefore Anselm's principle does not apply to it. It applies only to the most perfect conceivable being, which is defined as having eternal and independent (i.e., necessary) existence. Thus far, then, it would seem that his argument is able to withstand criticism.

Can Anselm's argument in its *first* form, however, be defended against Gaunilon's criticism? This depends upon whether the idea of the most perfect conceivable island is a coherent and consistent idea. Is it possible,

3 See p. 7.
4 Psalms 14:1 and 53:1.

even in theory, to specify the characteristics of the most perfect conceivable island? This is a question for the reader to consider for himself.

A second phase of the debate was opened when René Descartes (1596–1650), often called the father of modern philosophy, reformulated the argument and thereby attracted widespread attention to it.[5] Descartes brought to the fore the point upon which most of the modern discussions of the ontological argument have centered, namely, the assumption that existence is a property or predicate. He explicitly treats existence as a characteristic, the possession of which by a given *x* is properly open to inquiry. The essence or defining nature of each kind of thing includes certain predicates, and Descartes's ontological argument claims that existence must be included among the defining predicates of God. Just as the fact that its internal angles are equal to two right angles is a necessary characteristic of a triangle, so existence is a necessary characteristic of a supremely perfect being. A triangle without its defining properties would not be a triangle, and God without existence would not be God. The all-important difference is that in the case of the triangle we cannot infer that any triangles exist, since existence is not of the essence of triangularity. In the case of a supremely perfect being, however, we can infer existence, for existence is an essential attribute without which no being would be unlimitedly perfect.

This Cartesian version of the ontological argument was later challenged at two levels by the great German philosopher, Immanuel Kant (1724–1804).[6]

At one level he accepted Descartes's claim that the idea of existence belongs analytically to the concept of God, as the idea of having three angles belongs analytically to the concept of a three-sided plane figure. In each case the predicate is necessarily linked with the subject. But, Kant replied, it does not follow from this that the subject, with its predicates, actually exists. What is analytically true is that *if* there is a triangle, it must have three angles, and *if* there is an infinitely perfect being, he must have existence. As Kant says, "To posit a triangle, and yet to reject its three angles, is self-contradictory; but there is no self-contradiction in rejecting the triangle together with its three angles. The same holds true of the concept of an absolutely necessary being."

At a deeper level, however, Kant rejected the basic assumption upon which Descartes's argument rested, the assumption that existence, like

[5] *Meditations,* V. It is not entirely clear whether Descartes received the basic principle of his ontological argument from Anselm. When questioned by Mersenne about the relation of his own argument to Anselm's, he was content to reply "I will look at St. Anselm at the first opportunity." (N. Kemp Smith, *New Studies in the Philosophy of Descartes,* p. 304.) Descartes also presents another and different attempt to prove God's existence: *Discourse on Method,* IV and *Meditations,* III.

[6] Immanuel Kant, *Critique of Pure Reason,* tr. N. Kemp Smith (London: Macmillan & Company Ltd., 1933). "Transcendental Dialectic," Book II, Chap. 3, Sec. 4.

triangularity, is a predicate that something can either have or lack, and that may in some cases be analytically connected with a subject. He points out (as indeed the Scottish philosopher David Hume had already pointed out in a different context)[7] that the idea of existence does not add anything to the concept of a particular thing or kind of thing. An imaginary hundred dollars, for example, consists of the same number of dollars as a real hundred dollars. When we affirm that the dollars are real, or exist, we are merely *applying* the concept of the dollars to the world. Thus to say of *x* that it exists is not to say that in addition to its various other attributes it has the attribute of existing, but is to say that there is an *x* in the real world.

Essentially the same point has more recently been made by Bertrand Russell in his analysis of the word "exists."[8] He has shown that although "exists" is grammatically a predicate, logically it performs a different function, which can be brought out by the following translation: "Cows exist" means "There are *x*'s such that '*x* is a cow' is true." This translation makes it clear that to say that cows exist is not to attribute a certain quality (namely existence) to cows, but is to assert that there are objects in the world to which the description summarized in the word "cow" applies. Similarly "Unicorns do not exist" is the equivalent of "There are no *x*'s such that '*x* is a unicorn' is true." This way of construing negative existential statements — statements that deny that some particular kind of thing exists—avoids the ancient puzzle about the status of the "something" of which we can assert that it does not exist. Since we can talk about unicorns, for example, it is easy to think that unicorns must in some sense be or subsist or, perhaps, that they inhabit a paradoxical realm of non-being or potential being. Russell's analysis, however, makes it clear that "unicorns do not exist" is not a statement about unicorns but about the concept or description "unicorn," and is the assertion that this concept has no instances.

The bearing of this upon the ontological argument is as follows. If existence is, as Anselm and Descartes assumed, an attribute or predicate that can be included in a definition and which, as a desirable attribute, must be included in the definition of God, then the ontological argument is valid. It would be self-contradictory to say that the most perfect conceivable being lacks the attribute of existence. But, if existence, although it appears grammatically in the role of a predicate, has the quite different logical function of asserting that a description applies to something in reality, then the ontological argument, considered as a proof of God's

[7] David Hume, *A Treatise of Human Nature,* Book I, Part III, Sec. vii.

[8] This aspect of the theory of descriptions is summarized by Russell in his *History of Western Philosophy* (London: George Allen & Unwin Ltd., 1946), pp. 859–60. For a more technical discussion, see his *Introduction to Mathematical Philosophy* (1919), Chap. 16.

existence, fails. For if existence is not a predicate, it cannot be a defining predicate of God, and the question whether anything in reality corresponds to the concept of the most perfect conceivable being remains open to inquiry. A definition of God describes one's concept of God, but cannot prove the actual existence of any such being.

It should be added that some theologians, most notably Karl Barth, see Anselm's argument, not as an attempted proof of God's existence, but as an unfolding of the significance of God's revelation of himself as One whom the believer is prohibited from thinking as less than the highest conceivable reality. On this view, Anselm's argument does not seek to convert the atheist but rather to lead an already formed Christian faith into a deeper understanding of its object.[9]

The ontological argument has perennially fascinated the philosophical mind, and in recent years there have been a number of new discussions of it, some of the most important of which are listed in footnote 10.

THE FIRST CAUSE AND COSMOLOGICAL ARGUMENTS

The next important attempt to demonstrate the reality of God was that of Thomas Aquinas (1224/5–1274), who offers five ways of proving divine existence.[11] Unlike the ontological argument, which focuses attention upon the *idea* of God and proceeds to unfold its inner implications, Aquinas's proofs start from some general feature of the world around us and argue that there could not be a world with this particular characteristic unless there were also the ultimate reality which we call God. The first Way argues from the fact of motion to a Prime Mover; the second from causation to a First Cause; the third from contingent beings to a Necessary Being; the fourth from degrees of value to Absolute Value; and the fifth from evidences of purposiveness in nature to a Divine Designer.

We may concentrate upon Aquinas's second and third proofs. His second proof, known as *the First-Cause argument* is presented as follows: everything that happens has a cause, and this cause in turn has a cause, and so on in a series that must either be infinite or have its starting point in a first cause. Aquinas excludes the possibility of an infinite regress of

[9] See Karl Barth, *Anselm: Fides Quaerens Intellectum,* 1931 (London: Student Christian Movement Press Ltd. and Richmond, Va.: John Knox Press, 1960). Barth's interpretation is criticized by Etienne Gilson in "Sens et nature de l'argument de saint Anselme," *Archives d'histoire doctrinale et littéraire du moyen age,* 1934, pp. 23f.

[10] Charles Hartshorne, *The Logic of Perfection* (LaSalle, Ill.: Open Court Publishing Co., 1962), Chap. 2, and *Anselm's Discovery* (LaSalle Ill.: Open Court Publishing Co., 1965). Articles by Norman Malcolm, Jerome Shaffer, Arthur McGill, John Hick, and others are reprinted in *Many-Faced Argument.*

[11] Thomas Aquinas, *Summa Theologica,* Part I, Question 2, Art. 3. For an important recent philosophical study of Aquinas's arguments, see Anthony Kenny, *The Five Ways* (London: Routledge & Kegan Paul Ltd., 1969).

causes and so concludes that there must be a First Cause, which we call God. (His first proof, which infers a First Mover from the fact of motion, is basically similar.)

The weakness of the argument as Aquinas states it lies in the difficulty (which he himself elsewhere acknowledges)[12] of excluding as impossible an endless regress of events, requiring no beginning.

However, some contemporary Thomists (i.e., thinkers who in general follow Thomas Aquinas) have reinterpreted the argument in order to avoid this difficulty.[13] They interpret the endless series that it excludes, not as a regress of events back in time, but as an endless and therefore eternally inconclusive regress of explanations. If fact A is made intelligible by its relation to facts B, C, and D (which may be antecedent to or contemporary with A), and if each of these is in turn rendered intelligible by other facts, at the back of the complex there·must be a reality which is self-explanatory, whose existence constitutes the ultimate explanation of the whole. If no such reality exists, the universe is a mere unintelligible brute fact.

However, this reinterpretation still leaves the argument open to two major difficulties. First, how do we know that the universe is not "a mere unintelligible brute fact"? Apart from the emotional coloring suggested by the phrase, this is precisely what the sceptic believes it to be; and to exclude this possibility at the outset is merely to beg the question at issue. The argument in effect presents the dilemma: either there is a First Cause or the universe is ultimately unintelligible; but it does not compel us to accept one horn of the dilemma rather than the other.

Second (although there is only space to suggest this difficulty, leaving the reader to develop it for himself), the argument still depends upon a view of causality that can be, and has been, questioned. The assumption of the reformulated argument is that to indicate the causal conditions of an event is thereby to render that event intelligible. Although this assumption is true on the basis of some theories of the nature of causality, it is not true on the basis of others. If, for example, as much contemporary science assumes, causal laws state statistical probabilities,[14] or if (as Hume argued) causal connections represent mere observed sequences,[15] or are (as Kant suggested) projections of the structure of the human mind,[16] the Thomist argument fails.

12 Aquinas, *Summa Theologica,* Part I, Question 46, Art. 2. See also *Summa Contra Gentiles,* Book II, Chap. 38.

13 For example, E. L. Mascall, *He Who Is* (London: Longmans, Green & Co., 1943), Chap. 5.

14 Cf. Hans Reichenbach, *The Rise of Scientific Philosophy* (Berkeley: University of California Press, 1951), Chap. 10.

15 David Hume, *An Enquiry Concerning Human Understanding,* Sec. 7.

16 Kant, "Transcendental Analytic," in *Critique of Pure Reason.*

Aquinas's third Way, known as the argument from the contingency of the world, and often monopolizing the name *the cosmological argument*, runs as follows. Everything in the world about us is contingent—that is to say, it is true of each item that it might not have existed at all or might have existed differently. The proof of this is that there was a time when it did not exist. The existence of this page is contingent upon the prior activities of lumberjacks, transport workers, paper manufacturers, publishers, printers, author, and others, as well as upon the contemporary operation of a great number of chemical and physical laws; and each of these in turn depends upon other factors. Everything points beyond itself to other things. Saint Thomas argues that if everything were contingent, there must have been a time when nothing existed. In this case, nothing could ever have come to exist, for there would have been no causal agency. Since there are things in existence, there must be something that is not contingent, and this we call God.

Aquinas's reference to a hypothetical time when nothing existed seems to weaken rather than strengthen his argument. For there might be an infinite series of finite contingent events overlapping in the time sequence, so that no moment occurs that is not occupied by any of them. However, modern Thomists generally omit this phase of the argument (as indeed Aquinas himself does in another book).[17] If we remove the reference to time, we have an argument based upon the logical connection between a contingent world (even if this should consist in an infinite series of events) and its noncontingent ground. One writer points as an analogy to the workings of a watch. The movement of each separate wheel and cog is accounted for by the way in which it meshes with an adjacent wheel. Nevertheless, the operation of the whole system remains inexplicable until we refer to something else outside it, namely, the spring. In order for there to be a set of interlocking wheels in operation, there must be a spring; and in order for there to be a world of contingent realities, there must be a noncontingent ground of their existence. Only a self-existent reality, containing in itself the source of its own being, can constitute an ultimate ground of the existence of anything else. Therefore, if there is an ultimate ground of anything, there must be a "necessary being," and this "being" we call God.

The most typical philosophical objection raised against this reasoning in recent years is that the idea of a "necessary being" is unintelligible. It is said that only propositions, not things, can be logically necessary, and that it is a misuse of language to speak of a logically necessary *being*.[18] This

[17] Aquinas, *Summa Contra Gentiles,* Book II, Chap. 15, Sec. 6.

[18] See, for example, J. J. C. Smart, "The Existence of God" and J. N. Findlay, "Can God's Existence Be Disproved?" in *New Essays in Philosophical Theology,* eds. Antony Flew and Alasdair MacIntyre (New York: The Macmillan Company and London: Student Christian Movement Press Ltd., 1955).

particular objection to the cosmological argument is based upon a mis-apprehension, for the argument does not make use of the notion of a *logically* necessary being. The concept of a "necessary being," used in the main theological tradition (exemplified by both Anselm and Aquinas), is not concerned with logical necessity but rather with a kind of factual necessity which, in the case of God, is virtually equivalent to *aseity* or self-existence.[19] For this reason, the idea of God's "necessary being" should not be equated with the view that "God exists" is a logically necessary truth.

There remains, however, an important objection to the cosmological argument, parallel to one of those applying to the First-Cause argument. The force of the cosmological form of reasoning resides in the dilemma: *either* there is a "necessary being" *or* the universe is ultimately unintel-ligible. Clearly such an argument is cogent only if the second alternative has been ruled out. Far from being ruled out, however, this second alter-native represents the sceptic's position. This inability to exclude the possi-bility of an unintelligible universe prevents the cosmological argument from operating for the sceptic as a proof of God's existence—and the sceptic is, after all, the only person who needs such a proof.

Today there is an important neo-Thomist group of thinkers who hold that there are valid forms of the cosmological argument; some of the most important writings from this point of view are listed in footnote 20.

THE DESIGN   This has always been the most popular of the theistic
(OR TELEOLOGICAL)   arguments, tending to evoke spontaneous assent in
ARGUMENT   simple and sophisticated alike. The argument occurs
                        in philosophical literature from Plato's *Timaeus* on-
ward. (It appears again as the last of Saint Thomas's five Ways.) In modern times one of the most famous expositions of the argument from, or to, design is that of William Paley (1743–1805) in his *Natural Theology: or Evidences of the Existence and Attributes of the Deity Collected from the Appearances of Nature* (1802).[21] The argument is still in active commission, especially in more conservative theological circles.[22]

Paley's analogy of the watch conveys the essence of the argument. Sup-pose that while walking in a desert place I see a rock lying on the ground and ask myself how this object came to exist. I can properly attribute its presence to chance, meaning in this case the operation of such natural

19 See p. 7.

20 Mascall, *He Who Is,* Austin Farrer, *Finite and Infinite,* 2nd ed. (London: Dacre Press, 1960). See also Samuel M. Thompson, *A Modern Philosophy of Religion* (Chicago: Henry Regnery Co., 1955).

21 Paley's book has become available in an abridged version, ed. Frederick Ferré, in the Library of Liberal Arts, 1962.

22 For example, Robert E. D. Clark, *The Universe—Plan or Accident?* (Philadelphia: Muhlenburg Press, 1961).

forces as wind, rain, heat, frost and volcanic action. However, if I see a watch lying on the ground, I cannot reasonably account for it in a similar way. A watch consists of a complex arrangement of wheels, cogs, axles, springs, and balances, all operating accurately together to provide a regular measurement of the lapse of time. It would be utterly implausible to attribute the formation and assembling of these metal parts into a functioning machine to the chance operation of such factors as wind and rain. We are obliged to postulate an intelligent mind which is responsible for the phenomenon.

Paley adds certain comments that are important for his analogy between the watch and the world. First, it would not weaken our inference if we had never seen a watch before (as we have never seen a world other than this one) and therefore did not know from direct observation that watches are products of human intelligence. Second, it would not invalidate our inference from the watch to the watchmaker if we found that the mechanism did not always work perfectly (as may appear to be the case with the mechanism of the world). We would still be obliged to postulate a watchmaker. And third, our inference would not be undermined if there were parts of the machine (as there are of nature) whose function we are not able to discover.

Paley argues that the natural world is as complex a mechanism, and as manifestly designed, as any watch. The rotation of the planets in the solar system, and on earth the regular procession of the seasons and the complex structure and mutual adaptation of the parts of a living organism, all suggest design. In a human brain, for example, thousands of millions of cells function together in a co-ordinated system. The eye is a superb movie camera, with self-adjusting lenses, a high degree of accuracy, color-sensitivity, and the capacity to operate continuously for many hours at a time. Can such complex and efficient mechanisms have come about by chance, as a stone might be formed by the random operation of natural forces?

Paley (in this respect typical of a great deal of religious apologetics in the eighteenth century) develops a long cumulative argument drawing upon virtually all the sciences of his day. As examples of divine arrangement he points to the characteristics and instincts of animals, which enable them to survive (for example, the suitability of a bird's wings to the air and of a fish's fins to the water). He is impressed by the way the alternation of day and night conveniently enables animals to sleep after a period of activity. We may conclude with an example offered by a more recent writer, who refers to the ozone layer in the atmosphere, which filters out enough of the burning ultraviolet rays of the sun to make life as we know it possible on the earth's surface. He writes:

The Ozone gas layer is a mighty proof of the Creator's forethought. Could anyone possibly attribute this device to a chance evolutionary process? A wall which prevents death to every living thing, just the right thickness, and exactly the correct defense, gives every evidence of plan.[23]

The classic critique of the design argument occurs in David Hume's *Dialogues Concerning Natural Religion*. Hume's book was published in 1779, twenty-three years earlier than Paley's; but Paley took no account of Hume's criticisms—by no means the only example of lack of communication between theologians and their philosophical critics! Three of Hume's main criticisms are as follows.

1. He points out that any universe is bound to have the appearance of being designed.[24] For there could not be a universe at all in which the parts were not adapted to one another to a considerable degree. There could not, for example, be birds that grew wings but, like fish, were unable to live in the air. The persistence of any kind of life in a relatively fixed environment presupposes order and adaptation, and this can always be thought of as a deliberate product of design. The question, however, whether this order could have come about otherwise than by conscious planning remains to be answered. As an alternative, Hume suggests the Epicurean hypothesis: the universe consists of a finite number of particles in random motion. In unlimited time these go through every combination that is possible to them. If one of these combinations constitutes a stable order (whether temporary or permanent), this order will in due course be realized and may be the orderly cosmos in which we now find ourselves.

This hypothesis provides a simple model for a naturalistic explanation of the orderly character of the world. The model can be revised and extended in the light of the special sciences. The Darwinian theory of natural selection, for example, presents a more concrete account of the internal coherence of animal bodies and of their external adaptation to environment. According to Darwin's theory, animals are relatively efficient organisms in relation to their environment for the simple reason that the less well adapted individuals have perished in the continual competition to survive and so have not perpetuated their kind. The "struggle for survival," operating as a constant pressure toward more perfect adaptation, lies behind the evolution of life into increasingly complex forms, culminating in *homo sapiens*. To refer back to the ozone layer, the reason animal life on earth is so marvelously sheltered by this filtering arrangement is not that God first created the animals and then put the ozone layer in place to protect them, but rather that the ozone layer was there first, and only those forms of life capable of existing in the precise level of ultraviolet radiation that penetrates this layer have developed on earth.

[23] Arthur I. Brown, *Footprints of God* (Findlay, Ohio: Fundamental Truth Publishers, 1943), p. 102.

[24] Hume, *Dialogues Concerning Natural Religion,* Part VIII.

2. The analogy between the world and a human artifact, such as a watch or a house, is rather weak.[25] The universe is not particularly like a vast machine. One could equally plausibly liken it to a great inert animal such as a crustacean, or to a vegetable. But in this case the design argument fails, for whether crustaceans and vegetables are or are not consciously designed is precisely the question at issue. Only if the world is shown to be rather strikingly analogous to a human artifact, is there any proper basis for the inference to an intelligent Designer.

3. Even if we could validly infer a divine Designer of the world, we would still not be entitled to postulate the infinitely wise, good, and powerful God of Christian tradition.[26] From a given effect we can only infer a cause sufficient to produce that effect; and therefore, from a finite world we can never infer an infinite creator. To use an illustration of Hume's, if I can see one side of a pair of scales, and can observe that ten ounces is outweighed by something on the other side, I have good evidence that the unseen object weighs more than ten ounces; but I cannot infer from this that it weighs a hundred ounces, still less that it is infinitely heavy. On the same principle, the appearances of nature do not entitle us to affirm the existence of *one* God rather than many, since the world is full of diversity; or of a wholly *good* God, since there is evil as well as good in the world; nor, for the same reason, of a perfectly *wise* God or an unlimitedly *powerful* one.

It has, therefore, seemed to most philosophers that the design argument, considered as a proof of the existence of God, is fatally weakened by Hume's criticisms.

THEISM AND PROBABILITY

Since Hume's time a broader form of design argument has been offered by F. R. Tennant[27] and others, claiming that when we take account of a sufficiently comprehensive range of data—not only the teleological character of biological evolution but also man's religious, moral, aesthetic, and cognitive experience[28]—it becomes cumulatively more probable that there is a God than that there is not. Theism is presented as the most probable world-view or metaphysical system.

[25] *Dialogues,* Parts VI, VII.
[26] *Dialogues,* Part V. Cf. *An Enquiry Concerning Human Understanding,* Sec. XI, para. 105.
[27] F. R. Tennant, *Philosophical Theology,* II (Cambridge: Cambridge University Press, 1930), Chap. 4.
[28] Richard Taylor in *Metaphysics* (another volume in the Foundations of Philosophy Series), Chap. 7, makes striking use of man's cognitive experience in a reformulated design argument.

These thinkers claim that a theistic interpretation of the world is superior to its alternatives because it alone takes adequate account of man's moral and religious experience, as well as giving due place to the material aspects of the universe. Needless to say, this claim is disputed by nontheistic thinkers, who point in particular to the existence of evil as something that fits better into a naturalistic than into a religious philosophy. The problem of evil will be discussed in the next chapter; the question to be considered at the moment is whether the notion of probability can properly be applied to the rival hypotheses of the existence and the nonexistence of God.

Two main theories of probability, the "frequency" theory and the "reasonableness of belief" theory, are found in contemporary writings on the subject, developing what are sometimes called the statistical and inductive senses of probability. According to the first, probability is a statistical concept, of use only where there is a plurality of cases.[29] (For example, since a die has six faces, each of which is equally likely to fall uppermost, the probability of throwing any one particular number at a given throw is one in six.) As David Hume points out in his discussion of analogical reasoning, the fact that there is only one universe precludes our making probable judgments about it. If—impossibly—we knew that there were a number of universes (for example, ten) and if in addition we knew that (say) half of them were God-produced and half not, then we could deduce that the probability of our own universe being God-produced would be one in two. However, since by "the universe" we mean the totality of all that is (other than any creator of the universe), clearly no reasoning based upon the frequency theory of probability is possible concerning its character.

According to the other type of probability theory, to say that statement p is more probable than statement q is to say that when they are both considered in relation to a common body of prior (evidence-stating) propositions, it is more "reasonable" to believe p than q, or p is more worthy of belief than q.[30] The definition of reasonableness of course presents problems, but there is another special difficulty that hinders the use of this concept to assess the "theous" or "nontheous" character of the universe. In the unique case of the universe as a whole there is no body of prior evidence-stating propositions to which we can appeal, since all our propositions must be about either the whole or a part of the universe itself. In other words, there is nothing outside the universe which might count as evidence concerning its nature. There is only one universe, and it is capable of being interpreted both theistically and nontheistically.

[29] See, for example, Morris R. Cohen, *A Preface to Logic* (London: Routledge & Kegan Paul Ltd., 1946), Chap. 6.
[30] See, for example, Roderick M. Chisholm, *Perceiving* (Ithaca, N.Y.: Cornell University Press, 1957), Chap. 2.

It has been suggested that we may speak of "alogical" probabilities and may claim that in a sense that operates in everyday common-sense judgments, although it is not capable of being mathematically formulated, it is more likely or probable that there is than that there is not a God.[31] According to this view, the considerations that support the God-hypothesis are entitled to greater weight than those that suggest the contrary hypothesis. This, however, is clearly a question-begging procedure. For there are no common scales on which to weigh, for example, man's sense of moral obligation against the reality of evil, or his religious experience against the fact of human iniquity. Nor is there any valid sense in which it can be said that a religious interpretation of life is antecedently more probable than a naturalistic interpretation, or vice versa. Since we are dealing with a unique phenomenon, the category of probability has no proper application to it.

THE MORAL
ARGUMENT

The moral argument, in its various forms, claims that man's ethical experience, and particularly his sense of an inalienable obligation to his fellow human beings, presupposes the reality of God as in some way the source and ground of this obligation.

FIRST FORM

In one form the argument is presented as a logical inference from objective moral laws to a divine Law Giver; or from the objectivity of moral values or of values in general to a transcendent Ground of Values; or again, from the fact of conscience to a God whose "voice" is conscience —as in the following passage by Cardinal Newman:

If, as is the case, we feel responsibility, are ashamed, are frightened, at transgressing the voice of conscience, this implies that there is One to whom we are responsible, before whom we are ashamed, whose claims upon us we fear.... If the cause of these emotions does not belong to this visible world, the Object to which [the conscientious person's] perception is directed must be Supernatural and Divine....[32]

The basic assumption of all arguments of this kind is that moral values are not capable of naturalistic explanation in terms of human needs and desires, self-interest, the structure of human nature or human society, or in any other way that does not involve appeal to the Supernatural. To make such an assumption is to beg the question. Thus, an essential premise of the inference from axiology to God is in dispute, and from the point of view of the naturalistic sceptic nothing has been established.

[31] See, for example, Tennant, *Philosophical Theology*, I, chap. 11.
[32] J. H. Cardinal Newman, *A Grammar of Assent*, ed. C. F. Harrold, (New York: David McKay Co., Inc., 1947), pp. 83–84.

SECOND FORM

The second kind of moral argument is not open to the same objection, for it is not strictly a proof at all. It consists of the claim that anyone seriously committed to respect moral values as exercising a sovereign claim upon his life must thereby implicitly believe in the reality of a trans-human source and basis for these values, which religion calls God. Thus, Immanuel Kant argues that both immortality and the existence of God are "postulates" of the moral life, i.e., beliefs which can legitimately be affirmed as presuppositions by one who recognizes duty as rightfully laying upon him an unconditional claim.[33] Again, a more recent theological writer asks:

Is it too paradoxical in the modern world to say that faith in God is a very part of our moral consciousness, without which the latter becomes meaningless? . . . Either our moral values tell us something about the nature and purpose of reality (i.e., give us the germ of religious belief) or they are subjective and therefore meaningless.[34]

It seems to the present writer that so long as this contention is not over-stated it has a certain limited validity. To recognize moral claims as taking precedence over all other interests is, in effect, to believe in a reality, other than the natural world, that is superior to oneself and entitled to one's obedience. This is at least a move in the direction of belief in God, who is known in the Judaic-Christian tradition as the supreme moral reality. But it cannot be presented as a proof of God's existence, for the sovereign authority of moral obligation can be questioned, and even if moral values are acknowledged as pointing toward a transcendent ground they cannot be said to point all the way and with unerring aim to the infinite, omnipotent, self-existent, personal creator who is the object of biblical faith.

THE ARGUMENT FROM SPECIAL EVENTS AND EXPERIENCES It has also been claimed that various special happenings of a publicly observable kind, such as miracles and answers to prayer, establish the reality of God. It is doubtless true as a matter of psychological fact that a sufficiently impressive series of such happenings, if personally witnessed, would move almost anyone, however sceptical, to believe in God. But no general proof of divine existence, valid for those who have not experienced such events, can be based upon this fact. They can always either disbelieve the reports, for reasons classically stated by David Hume in his essay on *Miracles*,[35] or accept them but give them a naturalistic inter-

---

[33] *Critique of Practical Reason,* Book II, Chap. 2, Secs. 4 and 5.

[34] D. M. Baillie, *Faith in God and its Christian Consummation* (Edinburgh: T. & T. Clark, 1927), pp. 172–73.

[35] *An Enquiry Concerning Human Understanding,* Sec. X.

pretation. The new but potentially highly significant science of parapsychology has already greatly enlarged the range of naturalistic explanations of the "supernatural" for those who are willing to extend the sphere of the natural to include such phenomena as extrasensory perception (telepathy), awareness of future events (precognition), and even an alleged power of the mind to influence directly the movements of matter beyond the boundaries of one's own body (psychokinesis).

More private but still dramatic manifestations of God in vision and dream, by inner voice, numinous feeling, mystical or ecstatic experience have also convinced many of the reality of God. But once again it is not possible to found upon these experiences a general proof of divine existence. As the sceptical Thomas Hobbes remarked, when a man tells me that God has spoken to him in a dream, this "...is no more than to say he dreamed that God spake to him."[36] This point has been made again in recent philosophical critiques of the claim to meet the unseen God in a spiritual "I–Thou" encounter: although the believer has no doubt had the experience that he reports and that he regards as an I–Thou awareness of God, his having this experience does not guarantee the truth of his own interpretation of it. It may be that he had the experience described but that the correct explanation of it can be given by psychology rather than by theology.[37]

In short, any special event or experience which can be construed as manifesting the divine can also be construed in other ways, and accordingly cannot carry the weight of a proof of God's existence.

From this discussion, it is evident that the writer's own conclusion concerning the theistic proofs is negative. None of the arguments which we have examined seems qualified to compel belief in God in the mind of one who lacks that belief. However, it should be said in conclusion that many religious thinkers would disagree with this assessment and would hold that one or another of the traditional arguments, or several of them in combination, are rationally persuasive.

[36] *Leviathan*, Chap. 32.

[37] See, for example, C. B. Martin, *Religious Belief* (Ithaca, N.Y.: Cornell University Press, 1959), Chap. 5; and Ronald W. Hepburn, *Christianity and Paradox* (London: C. A. Watts & Company Ltd., 1958), Chaps. 3 and 4.

CHAPTER THREE

Grounds
for Disbelief in God

The responsible sceptic, whether agnostic or atheist, is not concerned with denying that religious people have had certain experiences as a result of which they have become convinced of the reality of God. The sceptic believes, however, that these experiences can be adequately accounted for without postulating a God, by adopting instead a naturalistic interpretation of religion. Two of the most influential such interpretations will now be discussed.

THE SOCIOLOGICAL THEORY OF RELIGION Developed mainly by French sociologists, principally Emile Durkheim,[1] earlier in the present century, this type of analysis appeals today to a generation which is acutely conscious of the power of society to mold for good or ill the minds of its members.

The sociological theory refers to this power when it suggests that the gods whom men worship are imaginary beings unconsciously fabricated

[1] *The Elementary Forms of the Religious Life,* 1912 (London: George Allen & Unwin Ltd., 1915).

by society as instruments whereby it exercises control over the thoughts and behavior of the individual.

The theory claims that when men have the religious feeling of standing before a higher power that transcends their personal lives and impresses its will upon them as a moral imperative, they are indeed in the presence of a greater environing reality. This reality is not, however, a supernatural Being; it is the natural fact of society. The encompassing human group exercises the attributes of deity in relation to its members and gives rise in their minds to the idea of God, which is thus, in effect, a symbol for society.

The sense of the holy, and of God as the source of sacred demand claiming the total allegiance of the worshiper, is thus accounted for as a reflection of society's absolute claim upon the loyalty of its members. In primitive societies (in relation to which Durkheim's theory was originally worked out) this sense of the group's right to unquestioning obedience and loyalty is very strong. The tribe or clan is a psychic organism, within which the human members live as cells, not yet fully separated as individuals from the group mind. The tribal customs, beliefs, requirements, and taboos are sovereign and bear collectively the awesome aspect of the holy. In advanced societies this primitive unity has enjoyed a partial revival in time of war, when the national spirit has been able to assert an almost unlimited authority over the citizens.

The key to the complementary sense of God as man's final succor and security is found in the way in which the individual is carried and supported in all the major crises of his life by the society to which he belongs. Man is social to the roots of his being, is deeply dependent upon his group, and is unhappy when isolated from it. It is the chief source of his psychic vitality, and he draws strength and reinforcement from it when as a worshiper he celebrates with his fellows the religion which binds them together ("religion" derives from the Latin *ligare,* to bind or bind together).

It is, then, society as a greater environing reality standing over against the individual, a veritable "ancient of days" existing long before his little life and destined to persist long after his disappearance, that constitutes the concrete reality which has become symbolized as God. This theory accounts for the symbolization that transforms the natural pressures of society into the supernatural presence of God by referring to a universal tendency of the human mind to create mental images and symbols.

Here, in brief, is an interpretation of the observable facts of religion that involves no reference to God as a supernatural Being who has created man and this world in which he lives. According to this interpretation, it is the human animal who has created God in order to preserve his own social existence.

Religious thinkers have offered various criticisms of this theory, perhaps the most comprehensive critique being that of H. H. Farmer.[2] The following difficulties have been stressed.

1. It is claimed that the theory fails to account for the universal reach of the religiously informed conscience, which on occasion goes beyond the boundaries of any empirical society and acknowledges a moral relationship to human beings as such. In the teaching of the great prophets and rabbis, and in the teaching of Jesus and of his church at its best, the corollary of monotheism has been pressed home: God loves *all* mankind and summons *all* men to care for one another as brothers.

How is this striking phenomenon to be brought within the scope of the sociological theory? If the call of God is only society imposing upon its members forms of conduct that are in the interest of that society, what is the origin of the obligation to be concerned equally for *all* men? Mankind as a whole is not a society as the term is used in the sociological theory. How, then, can the voice of God be equated with that of the group if this voice impels a man to extend to outsiders the jealously guarded privileges of the group?

2. It is claimed that the sociological theory fails to account for the moral creativity of the prophetic mind. The moral prophet is characteristically an innovator who goes beyond the established ethical code and summons his fellows to acknowledge new and more far-reaching claims of morality upon their lives. How is this to be accounted for if there is no other source of moral obligation than the experience of the organized group intent upon its own preservation and enhancement? The sociological theory fits a static "closed society"; but how can it explain the ethical progress that has come about through the insights of pioneers morally in advance of their groups?

3. It is claimed that the sociological theory fails to explain the socially detaching power of conscience. Again the criticism focuses upon the individual who is set at variance with his society because he "marches to a different drum"—for example, an Amos denouncing the Hebrew society of his time or, to span the centuries, an Alan Paton or a Father Huddleston rejecting the hegemony of his own race in South Africa, or again, Solzhenitsyn in Russia or Camilo Torres in Colombia. If the sociological theory is correct, the sense of divine support should be at a minimum or even altogether absent in such cases. The prophet cannot have the support of God against society if God is simply society in disguise. The record shows, however, that the sense of divine backing and support is often at a maximum in these situations. These men are sustained by a vivid sense of the call and leadership of the Eternal. It is striking that in one instance after another the Old Testament prophets express a sense of closeness to God

2 See H. H. Farmer, *Towards Belief in God* (London: Student Christian Movement Press Ltd., 1942), Chap 9, to which the present discussion is indebted.

as they are rejected by their own people; yet they belonged to an intensely self-conscious and nationalistic society of the kind that, according to the sociological theory, ought to be best able to impress its will upon its members.

It seems, therefore, that a verdict of "not proven" is indicated concerning this attempt to establish a purely natural explanation of religion.

THE FREUDIAN THEORY OF RELIGION   Sigmund Freud (1856–1939), the originator of psychoanalysis and a figure comparable in importance with Galileo, Darwin, or Einstein, devoted a good deal of attention to the nature of religion.[3] He regarded religious beliefs as ". . . illusions, fulfillments of the oldest, strongest, and most insistent wishes of mankind."[4] Religion, as Freud saw it, is a mental defense against the more threatening aspects of nature—earthquake, flood, storm, disease, and inevitable death. According to Freud, "With these forces nature rises up against us, majestic, cruel and inexorable."[5] But the human imagination transforms these forces into mysterious personal powers. "Impersonal forces and destinies [Freud said] cannot be approached; they remain eternally remote. But if the elements have passions that rage as they do in our own souls, if death itself is not something spontaneous but the violent act of an evil Will, if everywhere in nature there are Beings around us of a kind that we know in our own society, then we can breathe freely, can feel at home in the uncanny and can deal by psychical means with our senseless anxiety. We are still defenseless, perhaps, but we are no longer helplessly paralyzed; we can at least react. Perhaps, indeed, we are not even defenseless. We can apply the same methods against these violent supermen outside that we employ in our own society; we can try to adjure them, to appease them, to bribe them, and, by so influencing them, we may rob them of part of their power."[6] The solution adopted in Judaic-Christian religion is to project upon the universe the buried memory of our father as a great protecting power. The face that smiled at us in the cradle, now magnified to infinity, smiles down upon us from heaven. Thus, religion is ". . . the universal obsessional neurosis of humanity,"[7] which may be left behind when at last men learn to face

---

[3] See his *Totem and Taboo* (1913), *The Future of an Illusion* (1927), *Moses and Monotheism* (1939), *The Ego and the Id* (1923), and *Civilization and Its Discontents* (1930).

[4] *The Future of an Illusion. The Complete Psychological Works of Sigmund Freud,* trans. and ed. James Strachey (New York: Liveright Corporation and London: The Hogarth Press Ltd., 1961), XXI, 30.

[5] Freud, *Psychological* Works, XXI, 16.

[6] *Ibid.,* XXI, 16–17.

[7] *Ibid.,* XXI, 44.

the world relying no longer upon illusions but upon scientifically authenticated knowledge.

In *Totem and Taboo*, Freud uses his distinctive concept of the Oedipus complex[8] (which rests on concurrent ambivalent feelings) to account for the tremendous emotional intensity of man's religious life and the associated feelings of guilt and of obligation to obey the behests of the deity. He postulates a stage of human prehistory in which the unit was the "primal horde" consisting of father, mother, and offspring. The father, as the dominant male, retained to himself exclusive rights over the females and drove away or killed any of the sons who challenged his position. Finding that individually they could not defeat the father-leader, the sons eventually banded together to kill (and also, being cannibals, to eat) him. This was the primal crime, the parricide that has set up tensions within the human psyche out of which have developed moral inhibitions, totemism, and the other phenomena of religion. Having slain their father, the brothers are struck with remorse, at least of a prudential kind. They also find that they cannot all succeed to his position and that there is a continuing need for restraint. The dead father's prohibition accordingly takes on a new ("moral") authority as a taboo against incest. This association of religion with the Oedipus complex, which is renewed in each individual (for Freud believed the Oedipus complex to be universal), is held to account for the mysterious authority of God in the human mind and the powerful guilt feelings which make men submit to such a phantasy. Religion is thus a "return of the repressed."

There is an extensive literature discussing the Freudian treatment of religion, which cannot be summarized here.[9] The "primal horde" hypothesis, which Freud took over from Darwin and Robertson Smith, is now generally rejected by anthropologists,[10] and the Oedipus complex itself is

[8] Oedipus is a figure in Greek mythology who unknowingly murdered his father and married his mother; the Oedipus complex of Freudian theory is the child's unconscious jealousy of his father and desire for his mother.

[9] Some of the discussions from the side of theology are: R. S. Lee, *Freud and Christianity* (London: James Clarke Co. Ltd., 1948); H. L. Philip, *Freud and Religious Belief* (London: Rockliff, 1956); Arthur Guirdham, *Christ and Freud* (London: George Allen & Unwin Ltd., 1959); and from the side of psychoanalytic theory, T. Reik, *Dogma and Compulsion* (New York: International Universities Press, 1951); M. Ostow and B. Scharfstein, *The Need to Believe* (New York: International Universities Press, 1954); J. C. Flugel, *Man, Morals, and Society* (New York: International Universities Press, 1947).

[10] A. L. Kroeber, *Anthropology,* revised ed. (New York: Harcourt Brace Jovanovich, Inc., 1948), p. 616. Kroeber describes the psychoanalytic explanation of culture as "intuitive, dogmatic, and wholly unhistorical." Bronislaw Malinowski remarks in the course of a careful examination of Freud's theory, "It is easy to perceive that the primeval horde has been equipped with all the bias, maladjustments and ill-tempers of a middle-class European family, and then let loose in a prehistoric jungle to run riot in a most attractive but fantastic hypothesis." Bronislaw Malinowski, *Sex and Repression in Savage Society* (London: Routledge & Kegan Paul Ltd., 1927), p. 165.

no longer regarded, even by many of Freud's successors, as the key to unlock all doors. Philosophical critics have further pointed out that Freud's psychic atomism and determinism have the status not of observational reports but of philosophical theories.

Although Freud's account of religion, taken as a whole, is highly speculative, and will probably be the least-enduring aspect of his thought, his general view that faith is a kind of "psychological crutch" and has the quality of phantasy thinking is endorsed by many internal as well as external critics as applying to much that is popularly called religion. Empirical religion is a bewildering mixture of elements, and undoubtedly wish fulfillment enters in and is a major factor in the minds of many devotees.

Perhaps the most interesting theological comment to be made upon Freud's theory is that in his work on the father-image he may have uncovered the mechanism by which God creates an idea of himself in the human mind. For if the relation of a human father to his children is, as the Judaic-Christian tradition teaches, analogous to God's relationship to man, it is not surprising that human beings should think of God as their heavenly Father and should come to know him through the infant's experience of utter dependence and the growing child's experience of being loved, cared for, and disciplined within a family. Clearly, to the mind which is not committed in advance to a naturalistic explanation there may be a religious as well as a naturalistic interpretation of the psychological facts.

Again, it seems that the verdict must be "not proven"; like the sociological theory, the Freudian theory of religion *may* be true, but has not been shown to be so.

THE PROBLEM OF EVIL

To many, the most powerful positive objection to belief in God is the fact of evil. Probably for most agnostics it is the appalling depth and extent of human suffering, more than anything else, that makes the idea of a loving Creator seem so implausible and disposes them toward one or another of the various naturalistic theories of religion.

As a challenge to theism, the problem of evil has traditionally been posed in the form of a dilemma: if God is perfectly loving, he must wish to abolish evil; and if he is all-powerful, he must be able to abolish evil. But evil exists; therefore God cannot be both omnipotent and perfectly loving.

Certain solutions, which at once suggest themselves, have to be ruled out so far as the Judaic-Christian faith is concerned.

To say, for example (with contemporary Christian Science), that evil is an illusion of the human mind, is impossible within a religion based upon the stark realism of the Bible. Its pages faithfully reflect the characteristic mixture of good and evil in human experience. They record every kind of sorrow and suffering, every mode of man's inhumanity to man and of his painfully insecure existence in the world. There is no attempt to regard evil as anything but dark, menacingly ugly, heart-rending, and crushing. In the Christian scriptures, the climax of this history of evil is the crucifixion of Jesus, which is presented not only as a case of utterly unjust suffering, but as the violent and murderous rejection of God's Messiah. There can be no doubt, then, that for biblical faith evil is unambiguously evil and stands in direct opposition to God's will.

Again, to solve the problem of evil by means of the theory (sponsored, for example, by the Boston "Personalist" School)[11] of a finite deity who does the best he can with a material, intractable and coeternal with himself, is to have abandoned the basic premise of Hebrew-Christian monotheism; for the theory amounts to rejecting belief in the infinity and sovereignty of God.

Indeed, any theory that would avoid the problem of the origin of evil by depicting it as an ultimate constituent of the universe, co-ordinate with good, has been repudiated in advance by the classic Christian teaching, first developed by Augustine, that evil represents the going wrong of something that in itself is good.[12] Augustine holds firmly to the Hebrew-Christian conviction that the universe is *good*—that is to say, it is the creation of a good God for a good purpose. He completely rejects the ancient prejudice that matter is evil. There are, according to Augustine, higher and lower, greater and lesser goods in immense abundance and variety; but everything that has being is good in its own way and degree, except in so far as it may have become spoiled or corrupted. Evil—whether it be an evil will, an instance of pain, or some disorder or decay in nature—has not been set there by God, but represents the distortion of something that is inherently valuable. Whatever exists is, as such, and in its proper place, good; evil is essentially parasitic upon good, being disorder and perversion in a fundamentally good creation. This understanding of evil as something negative means that it is not willed and created by God; but it does not mean (as some have supposed) that evil is unreal and can be disregarded. On the contrary, the first effect of this doctrine is to accentuate even more the question of the origin of evil.

Theodicy,[13] as many modern Christian thinkers see it, is a modest enterprise, negative rather than positive in its conclusions. It does not claim to explain, nor to explain away, every instance of evil in human experience,

---

11 Edgar Brightman's *A Philosophy of Religion* (Englewood Cliffs, N.J.: Prentice-Hall, Inc., 1940), Chaps. 8–10, is a classic exposition of one form of this view.

12 See Augustine's *Confessions,* Book VII, Chap. 12; *City of God,* Book XII, Chap. 3; *Enchiridion,* Chap. 4.

13 The word "theodicy," from the Greek *theos* (God) and *dike* (righteous), means the justification of God's goodness in the face of the fact of evil.

but only to point to certain considerations that prevent the fact of evil (largely incomprehensible though it remains) from constituting a final and insuperable bar to rational belief in God.

In indicating these considerations it will be useful to follow the traditional division of the subject. There is the problem of *moral evil* or wickedness: why does an all-good and all-powerful God permit this? And there is the problem of the *nonmoral evil* of suffering or pain, both physical and mental: why has an all-good and all-powerful God created a world in which this occurs?

Christian thought has always considered moral evil in its relation to human freedom and responsibility. To be a person is to be a finite center of freedom, a (relatively) free and self-directing agent responsible for one's own decisions. This involves being free to act wrongly as well as to act rightly. The idea of a person who can be infallibly guaranteed always to act rightly is self-contradictory. There can be no certainty in advance that a genuinely free moral agent will never choose amiss. Consequently, the possibility of wrongdoing or sin is logically inseparable from the creation of finite persons, and to say that God should not have created beings who might sin amounts to saying that he should not have created people.

This thesis has been challenged in some recent philosophical discussions of the problem of evil, in which it is claimed that no contradiction is involved in saying that God might have made people who would be genuinely free but who could at the same time be guaranteed always to act rightly. A quote from one of these discussions follows:

> If there is no logical impossibility in a man's freely choosing the good on one, or on several occasions, there cannot be a logical impossibility in his freely choosing the good on every occasion. God was not, then, faced with a choice between making innocent automata and making beings who, in acting freely, would sometimes go wrong: there was open to him the obviously better possibility of making beings who would act freely but always go right. Clearly, his failure to avail himself of this possibility is inconsistent with his being both omnipotent and wholly good.[14]

A reply to this argument is indirectly suggested in another recent contribution to the discussion.[15] If by a free action we mean an action that is not externally compelled but that flows from the nature of the agent as he reacts to the circumstances in which he finds himself, there is indeed no contradiction between our being free and our actions being "caused"

[14] J. L. Mackie, "Evil and Omnipotence," *Mind* (April, 1955), p. 209. A similar point is made by Antony Flew in "Divine Omnipotence and Human Freedom," *New Essays in Philosophical Theology.* An important critical comment on these arguments is offered by Ninian Smart in "Omnipotence, Evil, and Supermen," *Philosophy* (April, 1961), with replies by Flew (January, 1962) and Mackie (April, 1962).

[15] Flew, in *New Essays in Philosophical Theology.*

(by our own nature) and therefore being in principle predictable. There is a contradiction, however, in saying that God is the cause of our acting as we do but that we are free beings *in relation to God*. There is, in other words, a contradiction in saying that God has made us so that we shall of necessity act in a certain way, and that we are genuinely independent persons in relation to him. If all our thoughts and actions are divinely predestined, however free and morally responsible we may seem to be to ourselves, we cannot be free and morally responsible in the sight of God, but must instead be his helpless puppets. Such "freedom" is like that of a patient acting out a series of posthypnotic suggestions: he appears, even to himself, to be free, but his volitions have actually been predetermined by another will, that of the hypnotist, in relation to whom the patient is not a free agent.

A different objector might raise the question of whether or not we deny God's omnipotence if we admit that he is unable to create persons who are free from the risks inherent in personal freedom. The answer that has always been given is that to create such beings is logically impossible. It is no limitation upon God's power that he cannot accomplish the logically impossible, since there is nothing here to accomplish, but only a meaningless conjunction of words[16]—in this case "person who is not a person." God is able to create beings of any and every conceivable kind; but creatures who lack moral freedom, however superior they might be to human beings in other respects, would not be what we mean by persons. They would constitute a different form of life that God might have brought into existence instead of persons. When we ask why God did not create such beings in place of persons the traditional answer is that only persons could, in any meaningful sense, become "children of God," capable of entering into a personal relationship with their Creator by a free and uncompelled response to his love.

When we turn from the possibility of moral evil as a correlate of man's personal freedom to its actuality, we face something that must remain inexplicable even when it can be seen to be possible. For we can never provide a complete causal explanation of a free act; if we could, it would not be a free act. The origin of moral evil lies forever concealed within the mystery of human freedom.

The necessary connection between moral freedom and the possibility, now actualized, of sin throws light upon a great deal of the suffering that afflicts mankind. For an enormous amount of human pain arises either from the inhumanity or the culpable incompetence of mankind. This includes such major scourges as poverty, oppression and persecution, war,

---

16 As Aquinas said, "...nothing that implies a contradiction falls under the scope of God's omnipotence." *Summa Theologica,* Part I, Question 25, Art. 4.

and all the injustice, indignity, and inequity that occur even in the most advanced societies. These evils are manifestations of human sin. Even disease is fostered to an extent, the limits of which have not yet been determined by psychosomatic medicine, by emotional and moral factors seated both in the individual and in his social environment. To the extent that all of these evils stem from human failures and wrong decisions, their possibility is inherent in the creation of free persons inhabiting a world that presents them with real choices followed by real consequences.

We may now turn more directly to the problem of suffering. Even though the major bulk of actual human pain is traceable to man's misused freedom as a sole or part cause, there remain other sources of pain that are entirely independent of the human will, for example, earthquake, hurricane, storm, flood, drought, and blight. In practice, it is often impossible to trace a boundary between the suffering that results from human wickedness and folly and that which falls upon mankind from without; both kinds of suffering are inextricably mingled together in human experience. For our present purpose, however, it is important to note that the latter category does exist and that it seems to be built into the very structure of our world. In response to it, theodicy, if it is wisely conducted, follows a negative path. It is not possible to show positively that each item of human pain serves a divine purpose of good; but, on the other hand, it does seem possible to show that the divine purpose as it is understood in Judaism and Christianity could not be forwarded in a world that was designed as a permanent hedonistic paradise.[17]

An essential premise of this argument concerns the nature of the divine purpose in creating the world. The sceptic's assumption is that man is to be viewed as a completed creation and that God's purpose in making the world was to provide a suitable dwelling-place for this fully formed creature. Since God is good and loving, the environment that he has created for human life to inhabit will naturally be as pleasant and comfortable as possible. The problem is essentially similar to that of a man who builds a cage for some pet animal. Since our world, in fact, contains sources of hardship, inconvenience and danger of innumerable kinds, the conclusion follows that this world cannot have been created by a perfectly benevolent and all-powerful deity.[18]

Christianity, however, has never supposed that God's purpose in the creation of the world was to construct a paradise whose inhabitants would experience a maximum of pleasure and a minimum of pain. The world is seen, instead, as a place of "soul making" or person making in which free beings, grappling with the tasks and challenges of their existence in a

[17] From the Greek *hedone,* pleasure.
[18] This is essentially David Hume's argument in his discussion of the problem of evil in his *Dialogues,* Part XI.

common environment, may become "children of God" and "heirs of eternal life." A way of thinking theologically of God's continuing creative purpose for man was suggested by some of the early Hellenistic Fathers of the Christian Church, especially Irenaeus. Following hints from Saint Paul, Irenaeus taught that man has been made as a person in the image of God but has not yet been brought as a free and responsible agent into the finite likeness of God, which is revealed in Christ.[19] Our world, with all its rough edges, is the sphere in which this second and harder stage of the creative process is taking place.

This conception of the world (whether or not set in Irenaeus's theological framework) can be supported by the method of negative theodicy. Suppose, contrary to fact, that this world were a paradise from which all possibility of pain and suffering were excluded. The consequences would be very far-reaching. For example, no one could ever injure anyone else: the murderer's knife would turn to paper or his bullets to thin air; the bank safe, robbed of a million dollars, would miraculously become filled with another million dollars (without this device, on however large a scale, proving inflationary); fraud, deceit, conspiracy, and treason would somehow always leave the fabric of society undamaged. Again, no one would ever be injured by accident: the mountain climber, steeplejack, or playing child falling from a height would float unharmed to the ground; the reckless driver would never meet with disaster. There would be no need to work, since no harm could result from avoiding work; there would be no call to be concerned for others in time of need or danger, for in such a world there could be no real needs or dangers.

To make possible this continual series of individual adjustments, nature would have to work by "special providences" instead of running according to general laws that men must learn to respect on penalty of pain or death. The laws of nature would have to be extremely flexible: sometimes gravity would operate, sometimes not; sometimes an object would be hard and solid, sometimes soft. There could be no sciences, for there would be no enduring world structure to investigate. In eliminating the problems and hardships of an objective environment, with its own laws, life would become like a dream in which, delightfully but aimlessly, we would float and drift at ease.[20]

One can at least begin to imagine such a world. It is evident that our present ethical concepts would have no meaning in it. If, for example, the notion of harming someone is an essential element in the concept of a wrong action, in our hedonistic paradise there could be no wrong actions— nor any right actions in distinction from wrong. Courage and fortitude

19 See Irenaeus's *Against Heresies*, Book IV, Chaps. 37 and 38.
20 Tennyson's poem, *The Lotus-Eaters*, well expresses the desire (analyzed by Freud as a wish to return to the peace of the womb) for such "dreamful ease."

would have no point in an environment in which there is, by definition, no danger or difficulty. Generosity, kindness, the *agape* aspect of love, prudence, unselfishness, and all other ethical notions which presuppose life in an objective environment could not even be formed. Consequently, such a world, however well it might promote pleasure, would be very ill adapted for the development of the moral qualities of human personality. In relation to this purpose it might be the worst of all possible worlds!

It would seem, then, that an environment intended to make possible the growth in free beings of the finest characteristics of personal life must have a good deal in common with our present world. It must operate according to general and dependable laws; and it must involve real dangers, difficulties, problems, obstacles, and possibilities of pain, failure, sorrow, frustration, and defeat. If it did not contain the particular trials and perils that—subtracting man's own very considerable contribution—our world contains, it would have to contain others instead.

To realize this is not, by any means, to be in possession of a detailed theodicy. It is to understand that this world, with all its "heartaches and the thousand natural shocks that flesh is heir to," an environment so manifestly not designed for the maximization of human pleasure and the minimization of human pain, may nevertheless be rather well adapted to the quite different purpose of "soul making."[21]

These considerations are related to theism as such. Specifically Christian theism goes further in the light of the death of Christ, which is seen paradoxically both (as the murder of the divine Son) as the worst thing that has ever happened and (as the occasion of man's salvation) as the best thing that ever happened. As the supreme evil turned to supreme good, it provides the paradigm for the distinctively Christian reaction to evil. Viewed from the standpoint of Christian faith, evils do not cease to be evils; and certainly, in view of Christ's healing work, they cannot be said to have been sent by God. Yet, it has been the persistent claim of those seriously and wholeheartedly committed to Christian discipleship that tragedy, though truly tragic, may nevertheless be turned, through a man's reaction to it, from a cause of despair and alienation from God to a stage in the fulfillment of God's loving purpose for that individual. As the greatest of all evils, the crucifixion of Christ, was made the occasion of man's redemption, so good can be won from other evils. As Jesus saw his execution by the Romans as an experience which God desired him to accept, an experience which was to be brought within the sphere of the

---

[21] This brief discussion has been confined to the problem of human suffering. The large and intractable problem of animal pain is not taken up here. For a discussion of it see, for example, Austin Farrer, *Love Almighty and Ills Unlimited* (Garden City, N.Y.: Doubleday & Company, Inc., 1961), Chap. 5, and John Hick, *Evil and the God of Love* (London: Collins, The Fontana Library, 1968), pp. 345–53.

divine purpose and made to serve the divine ends, so the Christian response to calamity is to accept the adversities, pains, and afflictions which life brings, in order that they can be turned to a positive spiritual use.[22]

At this point, theodicy points forward in two ways to the subject of life after death, which is to be discussed in later chapters.

First, although there are many striking instances of good being triumphantly brought out of evil through a man's or a woman's reaction to it, there are many other cases in which the opposite has happened. Sometimes obstacles breed strength of character, dangers evoke courage and unselfishness, and calamities produce patience and moral steadfastness. But sometimes they lead, instead, to resentment, fear, grasping selfishness, and disintegration of character. Therefore, it would seem that any divine purpose of soul making that is at work in earthly history must continue beyond this life if it is ever to achieve more than a very partial and fragmentary success.[23]

Second, if we ask whether the business of soul making is worth all the toil and sorrow of human life, the Christian answer must be in terms of a future good great enough to justify all that has happened on the way to it.

THE CHALLENGE OF MODERN SCIENCE

The tremendous expansion of scientific knowledge in the modern era has had a profound influence upon religious belief. Further, this influence has been at a maximum within the Judaic-Christian tradition, with which we are mainly concerned in this book. There has been a series of specific jurisdictional disputes between the claims of scientific and religious knowledge, and also a more general cumulative effect which constitutes a major element, critical of religion, in the contemporary intellectual climate.

Since the Renaissance, scientific information about the world has steadily expanded in fields such as astronomy, geology, zoology, chemistry, and physics; and contradicting assertions in the same fields, derived from the Bible rather than from direct observation and experiment, have increasingly been discarded. In each of the great battles between scientists and churchmen the validity of the scientific method was vindicated by its practical fruitfulness. Necessary adjustments were eventually made in the aspects

22 This conception of providence is stated more fully in John Hick, *Faith and Knowledge,* 2nd ed. (Ithaca, N.Y.: Cornell University Press, 1966), Chap. 10, some sentences from which are incorporated in this paragraph.

23 The position presented above is developed more fully in the author's *Evil and the God of Love,* 1966 (London: Fontana paperback ed., 1968). For an important philosophical critique of theodicies see Edward H. Madden and Peter H. Hare, *Evil and the Concept of God* (Springfield, Ill.: Charles C. Thomas, Publishers, 1968). Some of the most important recent articles on the subject are collected in Nelson Pike, ed., *God and Evil* (Englewood Cliffs, N.J.: Prentice-Hall, Inc., 1964).

of religious belief that had conflicted with the scientists' discoveries. As a result of this long debate it has become apparent that the biblical writers, recording their experience of God's activity in human history, inevitably clothed their testimony with their own contemporary prescientific understanding of the world. Advancing knowledge has made it possible and necessary to distinguish between their record of the divine presence and calling, and the primitive world view that formed the framework of their thinking. Having made this distinction, the modern reader can learn to recognize the aspects of the scriptures that reflect the prescientific culture prevailing at the human end of the divine–human encounter. Accordingly, we find that the three-storied universe of biblical cosmology, with heaven in the sky above our heads, hell in the ground beneath our feet, and the sun circling the earth but halting in its course at Joshua's command, is no longer credible in the light of modern knowledge. That the world was created some 6,000 years ago and that man and the other animal species came into being at that time in their present forms can no longer be regarded as a reasonable belief. Again, the expectation that at some future date the decomposed corpses of mankind through the ages will rise from the earth in pristine health for judgment has ceased to be entertained. Yet, in all of these cases, churchmen initially resisted, often with great vehemence and passion, scientific evidence that conflicted with their customary beliefs.[24] In part, this resistance represented the natural reaction of conservative-minded men preferring established and familiar scientific theories to new and disturbing ones. But this reaction was supported and reinforced by an unquestioning acceptance of the propositional conception of revelation (see pp. 51–54). This conception assumes that all statements in the scriptures are God's statements; consequently, to question any of them is either to accuse God of lying or to deny that the Bible is divinely inspired.

The more general legacy of this long history of interlocking scientific advance and theological retreat is the assumption, which is part of the characteristic climate of thought in our twentieth century western world, that even though the sciences have not specifically disproved the claims of religion, they have thrown such a flood of light upon the world (without at any point encountering that of which religion speaks) that faith can now be regarded only as a harmless private phantasy. Religion is seen as a losing cause, destined to be ousted from more and more areas of man's knowledge until at last it arrives at a status precisely akin to that of astrology—a cultural "fifth wheel," persisting only as a survival from previous ages in which our empirical knowledge was much less extensive.

The sciences have cumulatively established the autonomy of the natural

[24] The classic history of these battles is found in A. D. White, *A History of the Warfare of Science with Theology* (1896), 2 vols. This history is available in a paperback edition (New York: Dover Publications, Inc., 1960).

order. From the galaxies whose vastness numbs the mind to the unimag-
inably small events and entities of the subatomic universe, and throughout the endless complexities of our own world, which lies between these
virtual infinities, nature can be studied without any reference to God. The
universe investigated by the sciences proceeds exactly as though no God
exists.

Does it follow from this fact that there is, indeed, no God?

There are forms of theistic belief from which this negative conclusion
follows and others from which it does not.

If belief in the reality of God is tied to the cultural presuppositions of
a prescientific era, this set of beliefs, taken as a whole, is no longer valid.
But the situation is otherwise if we suppose (with much contemporary
theology) that God has created this universe, in so far as its creation relates
to man, as a neutral sphere in which his creatures are endowed with a
sufficient degree of autonomy to be able to enter into a freely accepted
relationship with their Maker. From this point of view, God maintains a
certain distance from man, a certain margin for a creaturely independence
which, although always relative and conditioned, is nevertheless adequate
for man's existence as a responsible personal being. This "distance" is
epistemic, rather than spatial. It consists in the circumstance that God, not
being inescapably evident to the human mind, is known only by means of
an uncompelled response of faith. (For a further elaboration of this idea,
see pp. 60–61). This circumstance requires that man's environment have
the kind of autonomy that, in fact, we find it to have. The environment
must constitute a working system capable of being investigated indefinitely
without the investigator being driven to postulate God as an element within
it or behind it. From the point of view of this conception of God, the autonomy of nature, as it is increasingly confirmed by the sciences, offers no
contradiction to religious faith. The sciences are exploring a universe that
is divinely created and sustained, but with its own God-given autonomy and
integrity. Such an understanding of God and of his purpose for the world is
able to absorb scientific discoveries, both accomplished and projected, which
have initially seemed to many religious believers to be profoundly threatening. The tracing back of man's continuity with the animal kingdom; the
locating of the origin of organic life in natural chemical reactions taking
place on the earth's surface, with the consequent prospect of reproducing
these reactions in the laboratory; the exploration of outer space and the
possibility of encountering advanced forms of life on other planets; the
probing of the chemistry of personality and the perfecting of the sinister
techniques of "brainwashing"; the contemporary biomedical revolution,
creating new possibilities for the control of the human genetic material
through, for example, gene deletion and cloning; the harnessing of nuclear
energy and the dread possibility of man's self-destruction in nuclear war—all

these facts and possibilities, with their immense potentialities for good or evil, are aspects of a natural order that possesses its own autonomous structure. According to religious faith, God created this order as an environment in which human beings, living as free and responsible agents, might enter into a relationship with God. All that can be said about the bearing of scientific knowledge upon this religious claim is that the claim does not fall within the province of any of the special sciences: science can neither confirm nor deny it.

From this theological point of view, what is the status of the miracle stories and the accounts of answered prayer that abound in the scriptures and in church records from the earliest to the present time? Must these be considered incompatible with a recognition that an autonomous natural order is the proper province of the sciences?

The answer to this question depends upon the way in which we define "miracle." It is possible to define the term in either purely physical and nonreligious terms, as a breach or suspension of natural law, or in religious terms, as an unusual and striking event that evokes and mediates a vivid awareness of God. If miracle is defined as a breach of natural law, one can declare a priori that there are no miracles. It does not follow, however, that there are no miracles in the religious sense of the term. For the principle that nothing happens in conflict with natural law does not entail that there are no unusual and striking events evoking and mediating a vivid awareness of God. Natural law consists of generalizations formulated retrospectively to cover whatever has, in fact, happened. When events take place that are not covered by the generalizations accepted thus far, the properly scientific response is not to deny that they occurred but to seek to revise and extend the current understanding of nature in order to include them. Without regard to the relevant evidence, it cannot be said that the story, for example, of Jesus healing the man with the withered hand (Luke 6:6–11) is untrue, or that comparable stories from later ages or from the present day are untrue. It is not scientifically impossible that unusual and striking events of this kind have occurred. Events with religious significance, evoking and mediating a vivid sense of the presence and activity of God, may have occurred, even though their continuity with the general course of nature cannot be traced in our present very limited state of human knowledge.

In the apologetic systems of former centuries miracles have played an important part. They have been supposed to empower religion to demand and compel belief. In opposition to this traditional view many theologians today believe that, far from providing the original foundation of religious faith, miracles presuppose such faith. The religious response, which senses the purpose of God in the inexplicable coincidence or the improbable and unexpected occurrence, makes an event a miracle. Thus, miracles belong to the internal life of a community of faith; they are not the means by which the religious community can seek to evangelize the world outside.[25]

The conclusion of this chapter is thus parallel to the conclusion of the preceding one. There it appeared that we cannot decisively prove the existence of God; here it appears that neither can we decisively disprove his existence.

---

[25] One of the best modern treatments of miracles is found in H. H. Farmer, *The World and God: A Study of Prayer, Providence and Miracle in Christian Experience,* 2nd ed. (London: Nisbet & Co., 1936). See also C. S. Lewis, *Miracles* (London: The Centenary Press, 1947).

CHAPTER FOUR

Revelation and Faith

THE LIMITS OF PROOF

We return now to our central question concerning the Judaic-Christian concept of God: what grounds are there for believing that any such being exists?

We saw in Chapters 2 and 3 that it is not possible to establish either the existence or the nonexistence of God by rational arguments proceeding from universally accepted premises. We saw also that arguments to the effect that theism is more probable than naturalism, or naturalism than theism, are basically defective, since the term "probable" lacks a precise meaning in this context.

In spite of the immense intellectual investment that has gone and is still going into the various attempts to demonstrate the existence of God, the conclusion, which many have reached, that this is indemonstrable agrees both with the contemporary philosophical understanding of the nature and limits of logical proof and with the biblical understanding of man's knowledge of God.

Philosophy recognizes two ways in which human beings may come to know whatever is to be known. One way (stressed by empiricism) is through experience, and the other (stressed by rationalism) is through reasoning. The limitation of the rationalist way is that the only truths capable of being strictly proved are analytic and ultimately tautological. We cannot by logic alone demonstrate any matters of fact and existence; these must be known through experience. That two and two equal four can be certified by strict proof; but that we live in a world of objects in space, and that there is this card table and that oak tree and those people, are facts that could never be known independently of sense perception. Indeed, if nothing were given through experience in its various modes we should never have anything to reason about. This is as true in religion as in other fields. God, if he exists, is not an idea but a reality outside us; therefore, if he is to be known to men, he must manifest himself in some way within their experience.

This conclusion is in line with the contemporary revolt against the rationalist assumptions which have dominated much of Western philosophy since the time of Descartes. Descartes held that we can only properly be said to know truths that are self-evident or that can be reached by logical inferences from self-evident premises. The still popular idea that to know means to be able to prove is a legacy of this tradition. Developing the implications of his starting point, Descartes regarded the reality of the physical world and of other people as matters that must be doubted until they have been established by strict demonstration. Perhaps, he suggested, all our sense experience is delusory. Perhaps, to go to the ultimate of doubt, there is an all-powerful malicious demon who not only deceives our senses but also tampers with our minds. In order to be sure that we are not being comprehensively deluded we should, therefore, doubt everything that can without self-contradiction be doubted and in this way discover if anything remains immune to our skepticism. There is one such indubitable item, namely, the fact that I who am now doubting exist: *cogito ergo sum* (I think, therefore I am). Building upon this immovable pinpoint of certainty, Descartes tried to establish, first the existence of God and then, through the argument that God would not allow us to be deceived, the veracity of our sense perceptions.[1]

One of Descartes's proofs of the existence of God, the ontological argument, was discussed in Chapter 2 and found wanting. And, indeed, even if that argument had seemed fully cogent, it would not provide an escape from a self-imposed state of Cartesian doubt. For the possibility that the "malicious demon" exists and has power over our minds undermines all proofs, since he can (by tampering with our memories) make us believe an argument to be valid which is in fact not valid. Really radical and thorough doubt can never be reasoned away, since it includes even our reasoning powers within its scope.

[1] Descartes, *Discourse on Method* and *Meditations*.

The only way of escaping radical doubt is to avoid falling into it in the first place. In the present century, under the influence of G. E. Moore (1873–1958) and others, the view has gained ground that Cartesian doubt, far from being the most rational of procedures, is perverse and irrational. It is, Moore protested, absurd to think that we need to prove the existence of the world in which we are living. For nothing is more certain to us than the reality of our physical environment. We start out with a consciousness of the world and of other people, and this consciousness is neither capable nor in need of philosophical justification.[2]

It has also been argued that when doubt becomes universal in its scope, it becomes meaningless. To doubt whether some particular perceived object is real is to doubt whether it is *as real as* the other sensible objects that we experience. "Is that chair really there?" means "Is it there in the way in which the table and the other chairs are there?" But what does it mean to doubt whether there is really anything whatever there? Such "doubt" is meaningless. For if nothing is real, there is no longer any sense in which anything can be said to be *un*real.

To put the same point slightly differently, if 'the word "real" has any meaning for us, we must acknowledge standard or paradigm cases of its correct use. We must be able to point to a clear and unproblematic instance of something being real. What can this be but some ordinary physical object perceived by the senses? But if tables and chairs and houses and people, etc. are accepted as paradigm cases of real objects, it becomes self-contradictory to suggest that the whole world of tables and chairs and houses and people may possibly be unreal. By definition, they are not unreal, for they are typical instances of what we mean by real objects.

To deny the validity of universal skepticism of the senses is not, however, to deny that there are illusions and hallucinations, or that there are many, and perhaps even inexhaustible, philosophical problems connected with sense perception. It is one thing to know that a number of sense reports are true, and another thing to discover the correct philosophical analysis of these reports.

This empiricist reasoning is in agreement with the unformulated epistemological assumptions of the Bible. Philosophers of the rationalist tradition, holding that to know means to be able to prove, have been shocked to find that in the Bible, which is the basis of Western religion, there is no attempt whatever to demonstrate the existence of God. Instead of professing to establish the reality of God by philosophical reasoning, the Bible

2 See G. E. Moore's papers "The Refutation of Idealism," reprinted in *Philosophical Studies* (London: Routledge & Kegan Paul Ltd., 1922); "A Defense of Common Sense," reprinted in *Philosophical Papers* (New York: The Macmillan Company, and London: Allen & Unwin, 1959); and *Some Main Problems of Philosophy* (New York: The Macmillan Company, and London: Allen & Unwins, 1953), Chap. 1.

takes his reality for granted. Indeed, to the biblical writers it would have seemed absurd to try to prove by logical argument that God exists. For they were convinced that they were already having to do with him, and he with them, in all the affairs of their lives. God was known to them as a dynamic will interacting with their own wills; a sheer given reality, as inescapably to be reckoned with as destructive storm and life-giving sunshine, or the hatred of their enemies and the friendship of their neighbors. They thought of God as an experienced reality rather than as an inferred entity. The biblical writers were (sometimes, though doubtless not at all times) as vividly conscious of being in God's presence as they were of living in a material environment. It is impossible to read their writings with any degree of sensitivity without realizing that to these people God was not a proposition completing a syllogism, or an abstract idea accepted by the mind, but the reality that gave meaning to their lives. Their pages resound and vibrate with the sense of God's presence as a building might resound and vibrate from the tread of some great being walking through it. It would be as sensible for a husband to desire a philosophical proof of the existence of the wife and family who contribute so much to the meaning in his life as for the man of faith to seek a proof of the existence of the God within whose purpose he is conscious that he lives and moves and has his being.

It is clear that from the point of view of a faith that is biblical in its orientation the traditional "theistic proofs" are irrelevant. Even if God could be validly inferred from universally accepted premises, this fact would be of merely academic interest to people who believe that they exist in personal relationship with God and already know him as a living presence. In order to consider the claims of those who worship, in Pascal's words, the "God of Abraham, God of Isaac, God of Jacob, not of the philosophers and scholars,"[3] we must investigate the claim that this God manifests himself within the sphere of human experience. The theological name for such alleged divine self-disclosure is "revelation," and for man's response to it, "faith."

THE PROPOSITIONAL VIEW OF REVELATION AND FAITH

Christian thought contains two very different understandings of the nature of revelation and, as a result, two different conceptions of faith (as man's reception of revelation), of the Bible (as a medium of revelation), and of theology (as discourse based upon revelation).

The view that dominates the medieval period and that is officially repre-

[3] The opening words of Pascal's Memorial, dated November 23rd, 1654, a confession of faith which was found after his death written on parchment and sewn in the lining of his coat.

sented today by Roman Catholicism (and also, in a curious meeting of opposites, by conservative Protestantism) can be called the "propositional" conception of revelation. According to this view, the content of revelation is a body of truths expressed in statements or propositions. Revelation is the imparting to man of divinely authenticated truths. In the words of the *Catholic Encyclopedia,* "Revelation may be defined as the communication of some truth by God to a rational creature through means which are beyond the ordinary course of nature."[4]

Corresponding to this conception of revelation is a view of faith as man's obedient acceptance of these divinely revealed truths. Thus faith is defined by the Vatican Council of 1870 as "a supernatural virtue whereby, inspired and assisted by the grace of God, we believe that the things which he has revealed are true." Or again, a contemporary American Jesuit theologian writes, "To a Catholic, the word 'faith' conveys the notion of an intellectual assent to the content of revelation as true because of the witnessing authority of God the Revealer...Faith is the Catholic's response to an intellectual message communicated by God."[5]

These two interdependent conceptions of revelation as the divine promulgation of religious truths, and of faith as man's obedient reception of these truths, are related to a view of the Bible as the place where those truths are authoritatively written down. They were first revealed through the prophets, then more fully and perfectly through Christ and the apostles, and are now recorded in the Scriptures. It is thus an essential element of this view that the Bible is not a merely human, and therefore fallible, record of divine truths. The First Vatican Council formulated Roman Catholic belief for the modern period by saying of the books of the Bible that "...having been written by inspiration of the Holy Ghost, they have God for their author." (One may compare with this statement the words of the Protestant evangelist, Dr. Billy Graham, "The Bible is a book written by God through thirty secretaries.") It should be added, however, that in Catholic theology Scripture is set within the context of tradition. Thus, the Council of Trent (1546–1563) declared that "...with the same devotion and reverence with which it accepts and venerates all the books of the Old and New Testament, since one God is the author of both, it also accepts and venerates traditions concerned with faith and morals as having been received orally from Christ or inspired by the Holy Spirit and continuously preserved in the Catholic Church." Protestantism on the other

---

4 *The Catholic Encyclopedia* (New York: Robert Appleton Co., 1912), XIII, 1.

5 Gustave Weigel, *Faith and Understanding in America* (New York: The Macmillan Company, 1959), p. 1. On the other hand, in some recent Catholic writings there is a growing tendency to recognize other aspects of faith as well as the element of intellectual assent. See, for example, Eugene Joly, *What is Faith?* (New York: Hawthorn Books, Inc., 1958).

hand recognizes no such oral tradition possessing equal authority with the Bible and claims that through the Bible God speaks directly to the Church as a whole and to the mind and conscience of individual believers.

This same propositional conception of revelation as God's imparting to men of certain truths that have been inscribed in the sacred Scriptures and are believed by faith, leads also to a particular view of the nature and function of theology. The propositional theory of revelation has always been accompanied by the distinction between natural and revealed theology. This distinction has been almost universally accepted by Christian theologians of all traditions until the present century. Natural theology was held to consist of all those theological truths that can be worked out by the unaided human intellect. It was believed, for example, that the existence and attributes of God and the immortality of the soul can be proved by strict logical argument involving no appeal to revelation. Revealed theology, on the other hand, was held to consist of those further truths that are not accessible to human reason and that can be known to us only if they are specially revealed by God. For example, it was held that although the human mind, by right reasoning, can attain the truth that God exists, it cannot arrive in the same way at the further truth that he is three Persons in one; thus the doctrine of the Trinity was considered to be an item of revealed theology, to be accepted by faith. (The truths of natural theology were believed to have been revealed also, for the benefit of those who lack the time or the mental equipment to arrive at them for themselves.)

Many modern philosophical treatments of religion, whether attacking or defending it, presuppose the propositional view of revelation and faith. For example, Professor Walter Kaufmann, in his lively and provocative *Critique of Religion and Philosophy,* assumes that the religious person who appeals to revelation is referring to theological propositions that God is supposed to have declared to mankind.[6] Indeed, probably the majority of recent philosophical critics of religion have in mind a definition of faith as the believing of propositions upon insufficient evidence.[7]

Many philosophical defenders of religion share the same assumption, and propose various expedients to compensate for the lack of evidence available to support their basic convictions. The most popular way of bridging the

[6] Walter Kaufmann, *Critique of Religion and Philosophy* (New York: Harper & Row, Publishers, 1958). For example, "Even if we grant, for the sake of the present argument, that God exists and sometimes reveals propositions to mankind..." (p. 89).

[7] For example, "The general sense is belief, perhaps based on some evidence, but very firm, or at least more firm, or/and of more extensive content, than the evidence possessed by the believer rationally warrants." C. J. Ducasse, *A Philosophical Scrutiny of Religion* (New York: The Ronald Press Company, 1953), pp. 73–74. Copyright 1953 by The Ronald Press.

evidential gap is by an effort of the will. Thus, one contemporary religious philosopher says that "...faith is distinguished from the entertainment of a probable proposition by the fact that the latter can be a completely theoretic affair. Faith is a 'yes' of self-commitment, it does not turn probabilities into certainties; only a sufficient increase in the weight of evidence could do that. But it is a volitional response which takes us out of the theoretic attitude."[8]

This emphasis upon the part played by the will in religious faith (an emphasis that goes back at least as far as Aquinas[9]) has provided the basis for a number of modern theories of the nature of faith, some of which will now be discussed.

VOLUNTARIST THEORIES OF FAITH

The classic treatments of religious faith as the acceptance of certain beliefs by a deliberate act of will are those of the seventeenth-century French thinker, Blaise Pascal, and the nineteenth-century American philosopher and psychologist, William James.

Pascal's "Wager" treats the question of divine existence as an enigma concerning which we can best take up our position on the basis of a calculation of risks. If we wager our lives that God exists, we stand to gain eternal salvation if we are right and to lose little if we are wrong. If, on the other hand, we wager our lives that there is no God, we stand to gain little if we are right but to lose eternal happiness if we are wrong. "Let us weigh the gain and the loss in wagering that God is. Let us estimate these two chances. If you gain, you gain all; if you lose, you lose nothing. Wager, then, without hesitation that He is."[10]

If we ask whether it is possible to make oneself believe in God, Pascal answers that this *is* possible—not indeed instantaneously, but by a course of treatment. "You would like to attain faith, and do not know the way; you would like to cure yourself of unbelief, and ask the remedy for it. Learn of those who have been bound like you...Follow the way by which they began; by acting as if they believed, taking the holy water, having masses said, etc. Even this will naturally make you believe, and deaden your acuteness (*et vous abêtira*)."[11]

Given an anthropomorphic (and to many people very unattractive) conception of God, Pascal's Wager amounts to a rational form of self-in-

---

[8] Dorothy Emmet, *The Nature of Metaphysical Thinking* (London: Macmillan & Company Ltd., 1945), p. 140.

[9] *Summa Theologica,* Second Part of the Second Part, Question 2, Art. 9.

[10] Pascal, *Pensées,* tr. F. W. Trotter (London: J. M. Dent & Sons Ltd., and New York: E. P. Dutton & Co., Inc., 1932), No. 233, p. 67.

[11] Pascal, *Pensées,* No. 233, p. 68.

surance. It assumes that God will be pleased by such a calculating and self-regarding attitude toward him. This assumption has seemed profoundly irreligious to many religious believers, although it has also been seriously adopted by others.[12]

William James (1842–1910), a founder of the pragmatist school, argues in his famous essay *The Will to Believe* (1897) that the existence or non-existence of God, of which there can be no conclusive evidence either way, is a matter of such momentous importance that anyone who so desires has the right to stake his life upon the God hypothesis. Indeed, we are obliged to bet our lives upon either this or the contrary possibility. "We cannot escape the issue by remaining skeptical and waiting for more light, because, although we do avoid error in that way *if religion be untrue,* we lose the good, *if it be true,* just as certainly as if we positively chose to disbelieve." James continues:

Better risk loss of truth than chance of error—that is your faith-vetoer's exact position. He is actively playing his stake as much as the believer is; he is backing the field against the religious hypothesis, just as the believer is backing the religious hypothesis against the field. To preach scepticism to us as a duty until "sufficient evidence" for religion be found, is tantamount therefore to telling us, when in presence of the religious hypothesis, that to yield to our fear of its being error is wiser and better than to yield to our hope that it may be true...Dupery for dupery, what proof is there that dupery through hope is so much worse than dupery through fear? I, for one, can see no proof; and I simply refuse obedience to the scientist's command to imitate his kind of option, in a case where my own stake is important enough to give me the right to choose my own form of risk.[13]

Further, if there is a personal God, our unwillingness to proceed on the supposition that he is real may make it impossible for us ever to be accepted by him: "...just as a man who in a company of gentlemen made no advances, asked a warrant for every concession, and believed no one's word without proof, would cut himself off by such churlishness from all the social rewards that a more trustworthy spirit would earn—so here, one who would shut himself up in snarling logicality and try to make the gods extort his recognition willy-nilly, or not get it at all, might cut himself off forever from his only opportunity of making the gods' acquaintance."[14]

The aspect of James's thought that is liable to strike one first is its complete lack of the kind of living religious faith that finds expression in the Bible. There is, Santayana said, "...no sense of security, no joy, in James's

---

[12] Pascal's Wager is used as an apologetic device by Edward J. Carnell, *An Introduction to Christian Apologetics* (Grand Rapids, Mich.: W. B. Eerdmans Publishing Co., 1948), pp. 357–59.

[13] William James in *The Will to Believe and Other Essays* (New York: Longmans, Green & Co., Inc., 1897), pp. 26–27.

[14] James in *The Will to Believe,* p. 28.

apology for personal religion. He did not really believe; he merely believed in the right of believing that you might be right if you believed."[15]

But the basic weakness of James's position is that it constitutes an unrestricted license for wishful thinking. James, at one point, imagines the Mahdi to write to us saying, "I am the Expected One whom God has created in his effulgence. You shall be infinitely happy if you confess me; otherwise you shall be cut off from the light of the sun. Weigh, then, your infinite gain if I am genuine against your finite sacrifice if I am not!"[16] The only reason that James could offer for not responding to this pressing invitation is that it did not rank as a "live option" in his mind. That is to say, it did not conform to the assumptions presently controlling his thinking. However, the fact that it was not a live option for James is an accidental circumstance that cannot affect the truth or falsity of the Mahdi's assertions. An idea might be true, although it did not appeal to William James; but if the idea were true, James would never come to know it by his method, which could only result in everyone becoming more firmly entrenched in their current prejudices. A procedure having this effect can hardly claim to be designed for the discovery of truth. It amounts to an encouragement to us all to believe, at our own risk, whatever we like. However, if our aim is to believe what is *true,* and not necessarily what we *like,* James's universal permissiveness will not help us.

A more recent philosophical theologian, F. R. Tennant, identifies faith with the element of willing venture in all discovery. He distinguishes faith from belief as follows.

Belief is more or less constrained by fact or Actuality that already is or will be, independently of any striving of ours, and which convinces us. Faith, on the other hand, reaches beyond the Actual or the given to the ideally possible, which in the first instance it creates, as the mathematician posits his entities, and then by practical activity may realize or bring into Actuality. Every machine of human invention has thus come to be. Again, faith may similarly lead to knowledge of Actuality which it in no sense creates, but which would have continued, in absence of the faith-venture, to be unknown: as in the discovery of America by Columbus.[17]

Tennant freely allows that there can be no general guarantee that faith will be justified. "Hopeful experimenting has not produced the machine capable of perpetual motion; and had Columbus steered with confidence for Utopia, he would not have found it."[18] Faith always involves risks; but it is only by such risks that human knowledge is extended. Science and

[15] George Santayana, *Character and Opinion in the United States* (Garden City, N.Y.: Doubleday & Company, Inc., Anchor Books, 1958), p. 47.

[16] James in *The Will to Believe,* p. 7.

[17] F. R. Tennant, *Philosophical Theology* (Cambridge: Cambridge University Press, 1928), I, 297. Tennant also expounded his theory in *The Nature of Belief* (London: The Centenary Press, 1943).

[18] Tennant, *Philosophical Theology,* I, 297.

religion are alike in requiring the venture of faith. "Science postulates what is requisite to make the world amenable to the kind of thought that conceives of the structure of the universe, and its orderedness according to quantitative law; theology, and sciences of valuation, postulate what is requisite to make the world amenable to the kind of thought that conceives of the why and wherefore, the meaning or purpose of the universe, and its orderedness according to teleological principles."[19]

Tennant's bracketing together of religious faith and scientific "faith" is highly questionable. A scientist's "faith" is significant only as a preliminary to experimental verification. It is often a necessary stage on the way to tested knowledge, and it has value only in relation to subsequent verification. But religious faith, according to Tennant, can hope for no such objective verification. In science, verification ". . . consists in finding that the postulate or theory is borne out by appeal to external facts and tallies with them."[20] But religious verification is of quite a different kind. It consists in the inwardly satisfying and spiritually fortifying effects of his faith upon the believer himself. "Successful faith. . . is illustrated by numerous examples of the gaining of material and moral advantages, the surmounting of trials and afflictions, and the attainment of heroic life, by men of old who were inspired by faith. It is thus that faith is pragmatically 'verified' and that certitude as to the unseen is established." However, even this purely subjective verification is undermined by the inevitable concession that ". . . such verification is only for [subjective] certitude, not a proving of [objective] certainty as to external reality. The fruitfulness of a belief or of faith for the moral and religious life is one thing, and the reality or existence of what is ideated and assumed is another. There are instances in which a belief that is not true, in the sense of corresponding with fact, may inspire one with lofty ideals and stimulate one to strive to be a more worthy person."[21] This admission reduces religious faith, as Tennant conceives it, to an unverifiable hope; and thereby undermines his attempt to assimilate religious to scientific cognition.

TILLICH'S CONCEPTION OF FAITH AS ULTIMATE CONCERN

Another conception of faith, differing from those so far mentioned, is that of Paul Tillich, who taught that "Faith is the state of being ultimately concerned."[22] Our ultimate concern is that which determines our being or not-being—not in the sense of our physical existence but in the sense of ". . . the reality, the structure, the

---

[19] Ibid. 299.

[20] Tennant, *The Nature of Belief*, p. 70.

[21] Ibid. p. 70.

[22] Paul Tillich, *Dynamics of Faith* (New York: Harper & Row, Publishers, 1957), p. 1.

meaning, and the aim of existence."[23] People are, in fact, ultimately concerned about many different things—for example, their nation or their personal success and status; but these are properly only preliminary concerns, and the elevation of a preliminary concern to ultimacy is idolatry. Tillich describes ultimate concern in an often quoted passage.

Ultimate concern is the abstract translation of the great commandment: "The Lord, our God, the Lord is one; and you shall love the Lord your God with all your heart, and with all your soul, and with all your mind, and with all your strength." The religious concern is ultimate; it excludes all other concerns from ultimate significance; it makes them preliminary. The ultimate concern is unconditional, independent of any conditions of character, desire, or circumstance. The unconditional concern is total: no part of ourselves or of our world is excluded from it; there is no "place" to flee from it. The total concern is infinite: no moment of relaxation and rest is possible in the face of a religious concern which is ultimate, unconditional, total, and infinite.[24]

This passage well exhibits the ambiguity of the phrase "ultimate concern," which may refer either to an *attitude* of concern or to the (real or imagined) *object* of that attitude. Does "ultimate concern" refer to a concerned state of mind or to a supposed object of this state of mind? Of the four adjectives that Tillich uses in this passage, "unconditional" suggests that it refers to an attitude of concern, "infinite" suggests that it refers to an object of concern, and "ultimate" and "total" could perhaps apply to either. From the pages of his *Systematic Theology,* it is indeed impossible to tell which meaning Tillich intends, or whether he has in mind both at once or sometimes one and sometimes the other.

In his later book, *Dynamics of Faith,* this ambiguity is resolved: Tillich explicitly adopts both of these two possible meanings by identifying the attitude of ultimate concern with the object of ultimate concern. "The ultimate of the act of faith and the ultimate that is meant in the act of faith are one and the same." This means the "...disappearance of the ordinary subject–object scheme in the experience of the ultimate, the unconditional."[25] That is to say, ultimate concern is not a matter of the human subject adopting a certain attitude to a divine Object but is, in Tillichian language, a form of the human mind's participation in the Ground of its own being. This notion of participation is fundamental to Tillich's thought. He contrasts two types of philosophy of religion, which he describes as ontological and cosmological.[26] The latter (which he associates with

---

[23] Paul Tillich, *Systematic Theology* (Chicago: Chicago University Press, 1951), I, 14. Copyright 1951 by the University of Chicago.

[24] Tillich, *Systematic Theology,* I, 11–12.

[25] Tillich, *Dynamics of Faith,* p. 11.

[26] "The Two Types of Philosophy of Religion," *Theology of Culture* (New York: Oxford University Press, Inc., 1959). Reprinted in John Hick, ed., *Classical and Contemporary Readings in the Philosophy of Religion* (Englewood Cliffs, N.J.: Prentice-Hall, Inc., 2nd ed., 1970).

Aquinas) thinks of God as being "out there," to be reached only at the the end of a long and hazardous process of inference; to find him is to meet a Stranger. For the ontological approach, which Tillich espouses and which he associates with Augustine, God is already present to us as the Ground of our own being. He is identical with us; yet at the same time he infinitely transcends us. Our finite being is continuous with the infinity of Being; consequently, to know God means to overcome our estrangement from the Ground of our being. God is not Another, an Object which we may know or fail to know, but Being-itself, in which we participate by the very fact of existing. To be ultimately concerned about God is to express our true relationship to Being.

As in the case of other elements in his system, Tillich's definition of faith as ultimate concern is capable of being developed in different directions. Stressing the removal of the subject–object dichotomy, his definition of faith can be seen as pointing to man's continuity or even identity with God as the Ground of his being. But it can also be seen as pointing in the opposite direction, toward so extreme a sundering of God and man that faith can operate as an autonomous function of the mind whether God be a reality or not. Tillich presents this view in the following passage.

"God"...is the name for that which concerns man ultimately. This does not mean that first there is a being called God and then the demand that man should be ultimately concerned about him. It means that whatever concerns a man ultimately becomes god for him, and, conversely, it means that a man can be concerned ultimately only about that which is god for him.[27]

Thus, with Tillich's formula, one can either define faith in terms of God, as man's concern about the Ultimate, or define God in terms of faith, as that—whatever it may be—about which man is ultimately concerned. This permissiveness between supranaturalism and naturalism is regarded by Tillich as constituting a third and superior standpoint "beyond naturalism and supranaturalism."[28] Whether Tillich is justified in regarding it in this way is a question for the reader to consider for himself.

A "NON-
PROPOSITIONAL"
VIEW OF
REVELATION
AND FAITH

A different view of revelation, which can be called in contrast the nonpropositional view (or, if a technical term is desired, the *heilsgeschichtliche* view), has become widespread within Protestant Christianity during the decades of the present century. This view claims to have its roots in the thought of the Reformers of the sixteenth century (Luther and Calvin and their associates)

[27] Tillich, *Systematic Theology*, I, 211.
[28] *Systematic Theology*, II, 5f.

and further back still in the New Testament and the early Church.[29]

According to this nonpropositional view, the content of revelation is not a body of truths about God, but God himself coming within the orbit of man's experience by acting in human history. From this point of view, theological propositions, as such, are not revealed, but represent human attempts to understand the significance of revelatory events. This nonpropositional conception of revelation is connected with the recent renewed emphasis upon the *personal* character of God, and the thought that the divine–human personal relationship consists in something more than the promulgation and reception of theological truths. Certain questions at once present themselves.

If it is God's intention to confront men with his presence, as personal will and purpose, why has he not done this in an unambiguous manner, by some overwhelming manifestation of divine power and glory?

The answer that is generally given runs parallel to one of the considerations that occurred in connection with the problem of evil. If man is to have the freedom necessary for a relationship of love and trust, this freedom must extend to the basic and all-important matter of his consciousness of God. God (as conceived in the Judaic-Christian tradition) is such that to be aware of him is, in important respects, unlike being aware of another finite person. The existence of a fellow human being can be a matter of indifference to us; it can "leave us cold." The obvious exception is that consciousness of another which is love. The peculiarly self-involving awareness of love bears a certain analogy to man's awareness of God. In love, the existence of the beloved, far from being a matter of indifference, affects one's whole being. God, the object of the religious consciousness, is such that it is impossible for a finite creature to be aware of him and yet remain unaffected by this awareness. God, according to the Judaic-Christian tradition, is the source and ground of our being. It is by his will that we exist. His purpose for us is so indelibly written into our nature that the fulfillment of this purpose is the basic condition of our own personal self-fulfillment and happiness. We are thus totally dependent upon God as the giver not only of our existence but also of our highest good. To become conscious of him is to see oneself as a created, dependent creature receiving life and well-being from a higher source. In relation to this higher Being, who has shown his nature to us as holy love, the only appropriate attitude is one of grateful worship and obedience. Thus, the process of becoming aware of God, if it is not to destroy the frail autonomy of the human personality, must involve the individual's own freely responding insight and assent.

---

[29] For an account of the development from the propositional to the nonpropositional view in modern Protestant thought, see John Baillie, *The Idea of Revelation in Recent Thought* (New York: Columbia University Press, 1956).

Therefore, it is said, God does not present himself to us as a reality of the same order as ourselves. If he were to do so, the finite being would be swallowed by the infinite Being. Instead, God has created space-time as a sphere in which we may exist in relative independence, as spatiotemporal creatures. Within this sphere God reveals himself in ways that allow man the fateful freedom to recognize or fail to recognize his presence. His actions always leave room for that uncompelled response that theology calls faith. It is this element in the awareness of God that preserves man's cognitive freedom in relation to an infinitely greater and superior reality. Faith is thus the correlate of freedom: faith is related to cognition as free will to conation. As one of the early Church Fathers wrote, "And not merely in works, but also in faith, has God preserved the will of man free and under his own control."[30]

Faith, conceived in this way as a voluntary recognition of God's activity in human history, consists in seeing, apperceiving, or interpreting events in a special way.

In ordinary nonreligious experience, there is something epistemologically similar to this in the phenomenon of "seeing as," which was brought to the attention of philosophers by Ludwig Wittgenstein (1889–1951) when he pointed out the epistemological interest of puzzle pictures.[31] Consider, for example, the page covered with apparently random dots and lines, which, as one gazes at it, suddenly takes the form of a picture of (say) a man standing in a grove of trees. The entire field of dots and lines is now seen as having this particular kind of significance and no longer as merely a haphazard array of marks.

We may well develop this idea, and add that in addition to such purely visual interpreting, there is also the more complex phenomenon of "experiencing as," in which a whole situation is experienced as having some specific significance. A familiar example of a situation that is perceived with all the senses and has its own practical significance is that of driving an automobile along a highway. To be conscious of being in this particular kind of situation is to be aware that certain reactions (and dispositions to react) are appropriate and others inappropriate; and an important part of our consciousness of the situation as having the particular character that it has consists in our readiness to act appropriately within it. Any individual would react in characteristically different ways in the midst of a battle and on a quiet Sunday afternoon stroll; he would do so in recognition of the differing characters of these two types of situation. Such awareness is a matter of "experiencing as." The significance of a given situation for a

---

[30] Irenaeus, *Against Heresies,* Book IV, Chap. 37, para. 5.
[31] Ludwig Wittgenstein, *Philosophical Investigations* (Oxford: Basil Blackwell, and New York: Mott Ltd., 1953), Part II, Sec. xi.

given observer consists primarily in its bearing upon his behavioral dispositions. Being an interpretative act, "experiencing as" can of course be mistaken, as—to mention an extreme case—when a lunatic feels that everyone is threatening him, and reacts accordingly.

Sometimes two different orders or levels of significance are experienced within the same situation; this is what happens when the religious mind experiences events both as occurring within human history and also as mediating the presence and activity of God. A religious significance is found superimposed upon the natural significance of the situation in the believer's experience.

Thus, for example, the Old Testament prophets saw the events of their contemporary history both as interactions between Israel and the surrounding nations and, at the same time, as God's dealings with his own covenant people—leading, guiding, disciplining, and punishing them in order that they might be instruments of his purpose. In the prophetic interpretation of history embodied in the Old Testament records, events which would be described by a secular historian as the outcome of political, economic, sociological, and geographical factors are seen as incidents in a dialogue that continues through the centuries between God and his people. It is important to realize that the prophets were not formulating a philosophy of history in the sense of an hypothesis applied retrospectively to the facts; instead, they were reporting their actual experience of the events as they happened. They were conscious of living in the midst of *Heilsgeschichte,* salvation–history. They saw God actively at work in the world around them. For example, a well-known commentary says of the time when the Chaldean army was investing Jerusalem, "Behind the serried ranks of the Chaldean army [Jeremiah] beheld the form of Jahwe fighting for them and through them against His own people."[32] The prophets experienced their contemporary situations as moments in which God was actively present.

The same epistemological pattern—the interpreting in a distinctive way of events that are in themselves capable of being construed either naturalistically or religiously—runs through the New Testament. Here again, in the story of a man, Jesus of Nazareth, and a movement which arose in connection with him, there are ambiguous data. It is possible to see him simply as a self-appointed prophet who got mixed up in politics, clashed with the Jerusalem priesthood, and had to be eliminated. It is also possible, with the New Testament writers, to see him as the Messiah of God, the one in whom the world was to witness the divine Son living a human life and giving himself for the renewing of mankind. To see him in this way

[32] John Skinner, *Prophecy and Religion* (Cambridge: Cambridge University Press, 1922), p. 261.

is to share the faith or the distinctive way of "experiencing as" which gave rise to the New Testament documents.[33]

This theme of God as *deus absconditus*, the hidden God, who comes to men in the incognito of the incarnation in order to preserve men's freedom in relation to himself, is found in Martin Luther, and is expressed with great clarity by Pascal.

It was not then right that He should appear in a manner manifestly divine, and completely capable of convincing all men; but it was also not right that He should come in so hidden a manner that He could not be known by those who should sincerely seek Him. He has willed to make Himself quite recognizable by those; and thus, willing to appear openly to those who seek Him with all their heart, and to be hidden from those who flee from Him with all their heart, He so regulates the knowledge of Himself that He has given signs of Himself, visible to those who seek Him, and not to those who seek Him not. There is enough light for those who only desire to see, and enough obscurity for those who have a contrary disposition.[34]

More broadly, religious apperception, within the Judaic-Christian tradition, experiences human life as a total situation in which men are at all times having to do with God and he with them. And the ethic which is an inseparable aspect of this faith indicates the way in which it is appropriate to behave in such a situation.

A CORRESPONDING VIEW OF THE BIBLE AND THEOLOGICAL THINKING
The conception of revelation as occurring in the events of history—both world history and men's personal histories—and of faith as the experiencing of these events as God's dealings with his human creatures also suggests a different conception of the Bible from that which accompanies the propositional theory. Within the propositional circle of ideas, the Bible is customarily referred to as "the Word of God." This phrase is understood in practice as meaning "the words of God." But within the contrasting set of ideas associated with the nonpropositional view of revelation, there is a tendency to return to the New Testament usage in which Christ, and only Christ, is called the divine Word (*Logos*). According to this view the Bible is not itself the Word of God but is rather the primary and indispensable witness to the Word. The New Testament

[33] This view of the nature of religious faith is presented more fully in my *Faith and Knowledge* (Ithaca, N.Y.: Cornell University Press, 2nd ed., 1966, Chaps. 5–6). This and many other topics in the epistemology of religion are illuminatingly discussed in Terence Penelhum, *Problems of Religious Knowledge* (London: Macmillan & Company Ltd., and New York: Herder & Herder, Inc., 1971).

[34] *Pensées*, tr. W. F. Trotter (London: J. M. Dent & Sons Ltd., and New York: E. P. Dutton & Co., Inc., 1932), No. 430, p. 118.

(upon which the discussions have mainly centered) is seen as the human record of the Incarnation, that is, of the "fact of faith" which is expressed in such statements as "the Word became flesh and dwelt among us, full of grace and truth; we have beheld his glory, glory as of the only Son from the Father."[35]

On the one hand, the Bible is a book written by men as the record of God's actions in history. It is, indeed, not so much *one* book as a library of books, produced during a period of about a thousand years and reflecting the various cultural situations within which its different sections were produced. In this sense it is a thoroughly human set of documents. On the other hand, the Bible is written from beginning to end from a standpoint of faith. Although it is the chronicle of a particular strand of world history that includes the settlement of a nomadic people in Canaan, the power struggle of kings, the rise and fall of dynasties and empires, and the changing patterns of economic and social life during some ten centuries, the Bible depicts these events as the scene of a continuing interaction between God and man. In the Bible, the chief agent upon the stage of history is not any human ruler, however powerful; it is the Lord who is invisible, yet ever present, never seen, yet never to be escaped, in one sense more remote than the farthest star but in another sense closer to a man than his own most secret thoughts. The faith of the biblical writers, which is their consciousness of God at work within human experience, constitutes the inspiration by virtue of which their writings still have the power to reveal the transcendent God to human consciousness. Paul Tillich has summed up a similar conception of the Scriptures.

The documentary character of the Bible is identical with the fact that it contains the original witness of those who participated in the revealing events. Their participation was their response to the happenings which became revealing events through their response. The inspiration of the biblical writers is their receptive and creative response to potentially revelatory facts. The inspiration of the writers of the New Testament is their acceptance of Jesus as the Christ, and with him, of the New Being, of which they became witnesses. Since there is no revelation unless there is someone who receives it as revelation, the act of reception is a part of the event itself. The Bible is both original event and original document; it witnesses to that of which it is a part.[36]

The nature of the Bible, as it is understood from the standpoint which we are now considering, is defined by the principle underlying the canon— that is, the principle by which the Christian Church decided which writings to include in its sacred Scriptures and which to exclude. As far as the Old Testament was concerned there was no problem, for the present collection of documents was already established and was simply taken over ready-made by Christianity. But the creation of a New Testament out of

[35] John 1:14.
[36] Tillich, *Systematic Theology,* I, 35.

the wealth of available material presented many problems. In addition to the contents of our present New Testament, there were in circulation a large number of writings, some now extant in full and others only in fragments, with such titles as *The Gospel According to the Hebrews, The Gospel of Philip, The Gospel of Peter, The Memoria of the Apostles, The Death of Pilate, The Assumption of the Virgin, The Martyrdom of Matthew.*[37] The series of practical discriminations and eventually of formal decisions by which the present canon of the New Testament was adopted has behind it a clear and highly significant principle. This is the principle of apostolic authority. The aim of the early Church was to gather, as far as was possible, all the writings that had come from the original band of Jesus' disciples, the twelve apostles, or from the circles that later grew up around some of them in different centers of the early Church. These apostolic writings—consisting chiefly of four memoirs of Jesus and a number of letters from the apostles and accounts of their activities—constituted the original and most nearly contemporary documentation of the momentous series of events in which, as the Christian community was convinced, the salvation of the world had been accomplished. Later critical investigation has questioned the judgment of the early Church at some relatively peripheral points;[38] but still the New Testament stands as essentially the original dossier of documents that were produced under the impact of the events out of which Christianity arose. It is through these writings that the revelatory events continue to make their impact upon mankind; and these writings, together with the Old Testament documents, constitute the given basis of Christian thought. Accordingly, it is not possible for Christian theology to go behind the scriptural data, taken in their totality.

It is clear, on this principle, why no later Christian writings, however profound, impressive, or uplifting, can ever rightly become included in the New Testament. For in the nature of the case, no later writings can be of apostolic origin. The only circumstance that could ever justify an enlargement of the canon to include books not now in it would be a discovery out of the sands and caves of the Middle East of ancient documents which, after the most careful scientific scrutiny, came to be accepted by the Church as authentic writings of the same category as the present contents of the New Testament—conceivably, for example, further letters by Saint Paul or the "lost ending" of Mark's Gospel.[39]

[37] These documents, together with many more in the same category, can be found in *The Apocryphal New Testament*, tr. M. R. James (Oxford: Clarendon Press, 1924).

[38] For example, critical investigation has questioned the Church's assumption that the Epistle to the Hebrews is by Saint Paul, and that the Gospel of John is by the apostle John.

[39] New Testament scholars are agreed that the present ending of Mark's Gospel, Chap. 16:9–20, is not part of the original document; and they conjecture that there may be a missing original ending.

The nonpropositional view of revelation also tends to be accompanied by a different conception of the function of theology from that operating in the propositional system of ideas. The strong emphasis upon God's self-revelation in and through the stream of saving history (*Heilsgeschichte*) recorded in the Bible, and upon the necessity for man's free response of faith, often leads to a rejection both of the distinction between natural and revealed theology and of the traditional conception of each member of this distinction. The notion of revealed theology is rejected on the ground that revelation means God disclosing *himself* (rather than a set of theological propositions) to man; and natural theology is rejected as a series of attempts to establish without faith what can only be given to faith.

This modern theological rejection of natural theology is not necessarily motivated by an irrationalist distrust of reason. It may represent an empiricism which recognizes that human thought can only deal with material that has been given in experience. Just as our knowledge of the physical world is ultimately based upon sense perception, so any religious knowledge must ultimately be based upon aspects of human experience that are received as revelatory. Thus, reason can never replace experience as the source of the basic religious data. Nevertheless, in its proper place and when allowed to fulfill its proper role, reason plays an important part in the religious life. Negatively, it can criticize naturalistic theories that are proposed as ruling out a rational belief in the reality of God; and in this way it may have the effect of removing blocks in the way of belief. Positively, it must seek to understand the implications of what is known by faith: in a famous phrase of Anselm's, this is "faith seeking understanding." And, of course, reason is at work also in the systematic formulation of what is believed on the basis of faith.

These latter functions of reason cover the work of the theologian. He takes the firsthand expressions of religious apperception, or faith, as data for careful and systematic reflection. His material consists in the fundamental "facts of faith" which constitute the experiential basis of a given religion. In the case of Christianity, for example, the central "fact of faith" is that expressed in Peter's words to Jesus, "You are the Christ, the Son of the living God."[40] Once certain "facts of faith" are acknowledged or confessed by a religious community, the task of its theologians is to draw out their implications, relating them both to one another and to human knowledge in other fields. The resulting theological formulations (according to the view which we are considering) have not been revealed by God, but represent human and therefore fallible attempts to understand the data of faith. The efforts of "faith seeking understanding" are a continuing part of the life of the Church, and have given rise to a rich variety of theological

[40] Matthew 16:16.

theories. In the endeavor to understand the "religious fact" of the Incarnation, for instance, many varieties of Christology have been and continue to be developed. There are divergent atonement theories to explain the reconciliation between man and God that is proclaimed in the Christian gospel; and there are also several different kinds of trinitarian doctrine to account for the threefold revelation of God pointed to in the New Testament.

It is important to distinguish between the assertion of "facts of faith" and the subsequent development of theological theories to explain them, for these fulfill distinct functions and have a different epistemological status. The "facts of faith" upon which a given religion is based define that religion and are (in intention at least) enshrined in its creeds. Theological theories, on the other hand, cannot claim the sanctity, within a particular religion, that is possessed by an affirmation of its basic "facts of faith." Much mental confusion, as well as ecclesiastical division, has been caused by attempts to treat the theological theories of some particular school as though they were themselves the basic articles of faith which they seek to explain. This kind of confusion is not unknown even today, as when the penal–substitutionary theory of the atonement is equated with the religious fact of man's reconciliation with God; or when the doctrine of the virgin birth of Jesus is equated with the Incarnation.

CHAPTER FIVE

Problems of Religious Language

THE PECULIARITY OF RELIGIOUS LANGUAGE

Contemporary work in the philosophy of religion has been much occupied with problems created by the distinctively religious uses of language. The discussions generally center around one or another of two main issues. One, which was familiar to medieval thinkers and which is being actively investigated with new philosophical techniques today, concerns the special sense that descriptive terms bear when they are applied to God. The other question, which also has a long history but which has been given fresh sharpness and urgency by contemporary analytical philosophy, is concerned with the basic function of religious language. In particular, do those religious statements that have the form of factual assertions (for example, "God loves mankind") refer to a special kind of fact—religious as distinguished from scientific fact—or do they fulfill a different function altogether? These questions will be discussed in the order in which they have just been mentioned.

It is obvious that many, perhaps all, of the terms that are applied in religious discourse to God are being used in special ways, differing from their use in ordinary mundane contexts. For example, when it is said that

"Great is the Lord . . . ," it is not meant that God occupies a large volume of space; when it is said that "the Lord spake unto Joshua," it is not meant that God has a physical body with speech organs through which he set in motion sound waves which impinged upon Joshua's eardrums. And when it is said that God is good, it is not meant that there are moral values independent of the divine nature, in relation to which God can be judged to be good; nor does it mean (as it commonly does of human beings) that he is subject to temptations but succeeds in overcoming them. There has clearly been a long shift of meaning between the familiar secular use of these words and their theological employment.

It is also clear that in all those cases in which a word occurs both in secular and in theological contexts, its secular meaning is primary in the sense that it developed first and has accordingly determined the definition of the word. The meaning that such a term bears when it is applied to God is an adaptation of its secular use. Consequently, although the ordinary, everyday meaning of such words as "good," "loving," "forgives," "commands," "hears," "speaks," "wills," "purposes" is relatively unproblematic, the same terms raise a multitude of questions when applied to God. To take a single example, love (whether *eros* or *agape*) is expressed in behavior in the speaking of words of love, and in a range of actions from lovemaking to the various forms of practical and sacrificial caring. But God is said to be "without body, parts, or passions." He has then, it would seem, no local existence or bodily presence through which to express love. But what is disembodied love, and how can we ever know that it exists? Parallel questions arise in relation to the other divine attributes.

THE DOCTRINE OF　　The great Scholastic thinkers were well aware of this
ANALOGY (AQUINAS)　problem and developed the idea of analogy to meet
　　　　　　　　　　　　it. The doctrine of "analogical predication" as it
occurs in Aquinas [1] and his commentator Cajetan,[2] and as it has been further elaborated and variously criticized in modern times, is too complex a subject to be discussed in detail within the plan of this book. However, Aquinas's basic and central idea is not difficult to grasp. He teaches that when a word, such as "good," is applied both to a created being and to God it is not being used *univocally* (i.e., with exactly the same meaning) in the two cases. God is not good, for example, in identically the sense in which human beings may be good. Nor, on the other hand, do we apply the epithet "good" to God and man *equivocally* (i.e., with completely

[1] *Summa Theologica,* Part I, Question 13, Art. 5; *Summa Contra Gentiles,* Book 1, Chaps. 28–34.
[2] Thomas De Vio, Cardinal Cajetan, *The Analogy of Names,* 1506 (Pittsburgh, Pa.: Duquesne University Press, 2nd ed., 1959).

different and unrelated meanings), as when the word "bat" is used to refer both to the flying animal and to the instrument used in baseball. There is a definite connection between God's goodness and man's, reflecting the fact that God has created man. According to Aquinas, then, "good" is applied to creator and creature neither univocally nor equivocally but *analogically*. What this means will appear if we consider first an analogy "downwards" from man to a lower form of life. We sometimes say of a pet dog that it is faithful, and we may also describe a man as faithful. We use the same word in each case because of a similarity between a certain quality exhibited in the behavior of the dog and the steadfast voluntary adherence to a person or a cause that we call faithfulness in a human being. Because of this similarity we are not using the word "faithful" equivocally (with totally different senses). But, on the other hand, there is an immense difference in quality between a dog's attitudes and a man's. The one is indefinitely superior to the other in respect of responsible, self-conscious deliberation and the relating of attitudes to moral purposes and ends. Because of this difference we are not using "faithful" univocally (in exactly the same sense). We are using it analogically, to indicate that at the level of the dog's consciousness there is a quality that *corresponds* to what at the human level we call faithfulness. There is a recognizable likeness in structure of attitudes or patterns of behavior that causes us to use the same word for both animal and man. Nevertheless, human faithfulness differs from canine faithfulness to all the wide extent that a man differs from a dog. There is thus both similarity within difference and difference within similarity of the kind that led Aquinas to speak of the *analogical* use of the same term in two very different contexts.

In the case of our analogy "downwards," true or normative faithfulness is that which we know directly in ourselves, and the dim and imperfect faithfulness of the dog is known only by analogy. But in the case of the analogy "upwards" from man to God the situation is reversed. It is our own directly known goodness, love, wisdom, etc., which are the thin shadows and remote approximations, and the perfect qualities of the God-head that are known to us only by analogy. Thus, when we say that God is good, we are saying that there is a quality of the infinitely perfect Being that corresponds to what at our own human level we call goodness. In this case, it is the divine goodness which is the true, normative, and unbroken reality, whereas human life shows at best a faint, fragmentary, and distorted reflection of this quality. Only in God can the perfections of being occur in their true and unfractured nature: only God knows, loves, and is righteous and wise in the full and proper sense.

Since God is hidden from us, the question arises of how we can know what goodness and the other divine attributes are in him? How do we know what perfect goodness and wisdom are like? Aquinas's answer is that we do not know. As used by him, the doctrine of analogy does not profess to spell out the concrete character of God's perfections, but only to indicate the relation between the different meanings of a word when it is applied both to man and (on the basis of revelation) to God. Analogy is not an instrument for exploring and mapping the infinite divine nature; it is an account of the way in which terms are used of the Deity whose existence is, at this point, being presupposed. The doctrine of analogy provides a framework for certain limited statements about God, without infringing upon the agnosticism, and the sense of the mystery of the divine being, which have always characterized Christian and Jewish thought at their best.

The conviction that it is possible to talk about God, yet that such talk can be carried to its destination only on the back of the distant analogy between the Creator and his creatures, is vividly expressed by the Catholic lay theologian, Baron von Hügel (1852–1925).[3] He speaks of the faint, dim, and confused awareness that a dog has of its master, and continues as follows.

The source and object of religion, if religion be true and its object be real, *cannot,* indeed, *by any possibility, be as clear to me even as I am to my dog.* For the cases we have considered deal with realities inferior to our own reality (material objects, or animals), or with realities level to our own reality (fellow human beings), or with realities no higher above ourselves than are we, finite human beings, to our very finite dogs. Whereas, in the case of religion—if religion be right—we apprehend and affirm realities indefinitely superior in quality and amount of reality to ourselves, and which, nevertheless (or rather, just because of this), anticipate, penetrate, and sustain us with a quite unpicturable intimacy. The obscurity of my life to my dog must thus be greatly exceeded by the obscurity of the life of God to me. Indeed the obscurity of plant life—so obscure for my mind, because so indefinitely inferior and poorer than is my human life—must be greatly exceeded by the dimness, for my human life, of God—of His reality and life, so different and superior, so unspeakably more rich and alive, than is, or ever can be, my own life and reality.[4]

RELIGIOUS STATEMENTS AS SYMBOLIC (PAUL TILLICH)

An important element in the thought of Paul Tillich is his doctrine of the "symbolic" nature of religious language.[5] Tillich distinguishes between a sign and a symbol. Both point to something else beyond themselves. But a sign signifies that to which it points by arbitrary convention—as for instance, when the red light at the street corner

---

[3] Friedrich von Hügel's principal works are the two volumes of *Essays and Addresses* and *The Mystical Element in Religion* and *Eternal Life,* each of which is a major classic on its subject.

[4] Friedrich von Hügel, *Essays and Addresses on the Philosophy of Religion,* First Series (New York: E. P. Dutton & Co., Inc. and London: J. M. Dent & Sons Ltd., 1921), pp. 102–3.

[5] This is to be found in Tillich's *Systematic Theology* and *Dynamics of Faith,* and in a number of articles: "The Religious Symbol," *Journal of Liberal Religion,* II,

signifies that drivers are ordered to halt. In contrast to this purely external connection, a symbol "participates in that to which it points."[6] To use Tillich's example, a flag participates in the power and dignity of the nation that it represents. Because of this inner connection with the reality symbolized, symbols are not arbitrarily instituted, like conventional signs, but "grow out of the individual or collective unconscious"[7] and consequently have their own span of life and (in some cases) their decay and death. A symbol "opens up levels of reality which otherwise are closed to us" and at the same time "unlocks dimensions and elements of our soul"[8] corresponding to the new aspects of the world that it reveals. The clearest instances of this twofold function are provided by the arts, which "create symbols for a level of reality which cannot be reached in any other way,"[9] at the same time opening up new sensitivities and powers of appreciation in ourselves.

Tillich holds that religious faith, which is the state of being "ultimately concerned" about the ultimate, can only express itself in symbolic language. "Whatever we say about that which concerns us ultimately, whether or not we call it God, has a symbolic meaning. It points beyond itself while participating in that to which it points. In no other way can faith express itself adequately. The language of faith is the language of symbols."[10]

There is, according to Tillich, one and only one literal, nonsymbolic statement that can be made about the ultimate reality which religion calls God—that God is Being-itself. Beyond this, all theological statements—such as, that God is eternal, living, good, personal, that he is the Creator and that he loves his creatures—are symbolic.

There can be no doubt that any concrete assertion about God must be symbolic, for a concrete assertion is one which uses a segment of finite experience in order to say something about him. It transcends the content of this segment, although

---

No. 1 (Summer, 1940); "Religious Symbols and our Knowledge of God," *The Christian Scholar,* XXXVIII, No. 3 (September, 1955); "Theology and Symbolism," *Religious Symbolism,* ed. F. E. Johnson (New York: Harper & Row, Publishers, 1955); "Existential Analyses and Religious Symbols," *Contemporary Problems in Religion,* ed. Harold A. Basilius (Detroit: Wayne State University Press, 1956), reprinted in *Four Existentialist Theologians,* ed. Will Herberg (Garden City, N.Y.: Doubleday & Company, Inc., Anchor Books, 1958); "The Word of God," *Language,* ed. Ruth Anshen (New York: Harper & Row, Publishers, 1957). For a philosophical critique of Tillich's doctrine of religious symbols, see William Alston, "Tillich's Conception of a Religious Symbol," *Religious Experience and Truth,* ed. Sidney Hook (New York: New York University Press, 1961), which volume also contains two further essays by Tillich, "The Religious Symbol" and "The Meaning and Justification of Religious Symbols."

[6] Paul Tillich, *Dynamics of Faith* (New York: Harper & Row, Publishers), p. 42.

[7] Ibid., p. 43.

[8] Ibid., p. 42.

[9] Ibid., p. 42.

[10] Ibid., p. 45.

it also includes it. The segment of finite reality which becomes the vehicle of a concrete assertion about God is affirmed and negated at the same time. It becomes a symbol, for a symbolic expression is one whose proper meaning is negated by that to which it points. And yet it also is affirmed by it, and this affirmation gives the symbolic expression an adequate basis for pointing beyond itself.[11]

Tillich's conception of the symbolic character of religious language can—like many of his central ideas—be developed in either of two opposite directions and is presented by Tillich in the body of his writings as a whole in such a way as to preserve its ambiguity and flexibility. I shall, at this point, consider Tillich's doctrine in its theistic development, indicating in a later section, in connection with the view of J. H. Randall, Jr., how it can also be developed naturalistically.[12]

Used in the service of Judaic-Christian theism, the negative aspect of Tillich's doctrine of religious symbols corresponds to the negative aspect of the doctrine of analogy. Tillich is insisting that we do not use human language literally, or univocally, when we speak of the ultimate. Because our terms can only be derived from our own finite human experience, they cannot be adequate to apply to God; when used theologically, their meaning is always partially "negated by that to which they point." Religiously, this doctrine constitutes a warning against the idolatry of thinking of God as though he were merely a greatly magnified human being (anthropomorphism).

Tillich's constructive teaching, offering an alternative to the doctrine of analogy, is his theory of "participation." A symbol, he says, participates in the reality to which it points. But unfortunately Tillich does not define or clarify this central notion of participation. Consider, for example, the symbolic statement that God is good. Is the symbol in this case the proposition "God is good," or the concept "the goodness of God"? Does this symbol participate in Being-itself in the same sense as that in which a flag participates in the power and dignity of a nation? And what precisely is this sense? Tillich does not analyze the latter case—which he uses in several different places to indicate what he means by the participation of a symbol in that which it symbolizes. Consequently, it is not clear in what respect the case of a religious symbol is supposed to be similar. Again, according to Tillich, everything that exists participates in Being-itself; what then is the difference between the way in which symbols participate in Being-itself and the way in which everything else participates in it?

The application to theological statements of Tillich's other "main characteristics of every symbol,"[13] summarized above, raises further questions. Is it really plausible to say that a complex theological statement such as

11 Tillich, *Systematic Theology*, I, 239.
12 See pp. 76–77.
13 Tillich, *Dynamics of Faith*, p. 43.

"God is not dependent for his existence upon any reality other than himself" has arisen from the unconscious, whether individual or collective? Does it not seem more likely that it was carefully formulated by a philosophical theologian? And in what sense does this same proposition open up both "levels of reality which are otherwise closed to us" and "hidden depths of our own being"? These two characteristics of symbols seem more readily applicable to the arts than to theological ideas and propositions. Indeed, it is Tillich's tendency to assimilate religious to aesthetic awareness that suggests the naturalistic development of his position, which will be described later (pp. 76–77).

These are some of the many questions that Tillich's position raises. In default of answers to such questions, Tillich's teaching, although valuably suggestive, scarcely constitutes at this point a fully articulated philosophical position.

INCARNATION
AND THE PROBLEM
OF MEANING

It is claimed by some that the doctrine of the Incarnation (which together with all that follows from it distinguishes Christianity from Judaism) offers the possibility of a partial solution to the problem of theological meaning. There is a longstanding distinction between the metaphysical attributes of God (aseity, eternity, infinity, etc.) and his moral attributes (goodness, love, wisdom etc.). The doctrine of the Incarnation involves the claim that the moral (but not the metaphysical) attributes of God have been embodied, so far as this is possible, in a finite human life, namely that of the Christ. This claim makes it possible to point to the person of Christ as showing what is meant by assertions such as "God is good" and "God loves his human creatures." The moral attitudes of God toward mankind are held to have been incarnated in Jesus and expressed concretely in his dealings with men and women. The Incarnation doctrine involves the claim that, for example, Jesus' compassion for the sick and the spiritually blind was God's compassion for them; his forgiving of sins, God's forgiveness; and his condemnation of the self-righteously religious, God's condemnation of them. On the basis of this belief, the life of Christ as depicted in the New Testament records provides a foundation for statements about God. From God's attitudes in Christ toward a random assortment of men and women in first-century Palestine, it is possible to affirm, for example, that God's love is continuous in character with that displayed in the life of Jesus.[14]

The doctrine of the Incarnation is used in relation to the same problem in a somewhat different way by Ian Crombie. "What we do [he says in the

[14] For a criticism of this view, see Ronald Hepburn, *Christianity and Paradox* (London. C. A. Watts & Company Ltd., 1958), Chap. 5.

course of an illuminating discussion of the problem of theological meaning]
is in essence to think of God in parables." He continues as follows:

> The things we say about God are said on the authority of the words and acts
> of Christ, who spoke in human language, using parable; and so we too speak
> of God in parable—authoritative parable, authorized parable; knowing that the
> truth is not literally that which our parables represent, knowing therefore that
> now we see in a glass darkly, but trusting, because we trust the source of the
> parables, that in believing them and interpreting them in the light of each
> other, we shall not be misled, that we shall have such knowledge as we need to
> possess for the foundation of the religious life.[15]

RELIGIOUS
LANGUAGE AS
NONCOGNITIVE

When we assert what we take to be a fact (or deny
what is alleged to be a fact) we are using language
cognitively. "The population of China is 650,000,000,"
"This is a hot summer," "Two plus two equal four,"
"He is not here" are cognitive utterances. Indeed, we can define a cognitive
(or informative or indicative) sentence as one that is either true or false.

But there are other types of utterance that are neither true nor false,
because they fulfill quite a different function from that of endeavoring to
describe facts. We do not ask of a swearword, or a command, or the
baptismal formula, or a sonnet whether it is true. The function of the
swearword is to vent one's feelings; of the command, to direct someone's
actions; of "I baptize thee . . . ," to perform a baptism; of the sonnet, to
evoke emotions and mental images. The question arises whether theological
sentences, such as "God loves mankind," are cognitive or noncognitive. This
query at once divides into two: 1. Are such sentences intended by their
users to be construed cognitively? 2. Is their logical character such that they
can, in fact, regardless of intention, be either true or false? The first of
these questions will be discussed in the present and the second in the following chapter.

There is no doubt that as a matter of historical fact religious people
have normally believed such statements as "God loves mankind" to be not
only cognitive but also true. Without necessarily pausing to consider the
difference between religious facts and the facts disclosed through sense
perception and the sciences, ordinary believers within the Judaic-Christian
tradition have assumed that there are religious realities and facts, and that
their own religious convictions are concerned with such.

Today, however, a growing number of theories treat religious language
as noncognitive. Two of these theories, of somewhat different types, will

---

15 "Theology and Falsification," *New Essays in Philosophical Theology,* eds. Antony Flew and Alasdair MacIntyre, pp. 122–23. See also Ian Crombie's article, "The
Possibility of Theological Statements" in *Faith and Logic,* ed. Basil Mitchell (London: George Allen & Unwin Ltd., 1957).

now be described. A clear statement of the first type comes from Professor J. H. Randall, Jr. in his book, *The Role of Knowledge in Western Religion*.[16] His exposition indicates, incidentally, how a view of religious symbols that is very close to Tillich's can be used in the service of naturalism.[17]

Randall conceives of religion as a human activity which, like its compeers, science and art, makes its own special contribution to man's culture. The distinctive material with which religion works is a body of symbols and myths. "What is important to recognize [says Randall] is that religious symbols belong with social and artistic symbols, in the group of symbols that are both *nonrepresentative* and *noncognitive*. Such noncognitive symbols can be said to symbolize not some external thing that can be indicated apart from their operation, but rather what they themselves *do*, their peculiar functions."[18]

According to Randall, religious symbols have a fourfold function. First, they arouse the emotions and stir men to actions; they may thereby strengthen men's practical commitment to what they believe to be right. Second, they stimulate cooperative action and thus bind a community together through a common response to its symbols. Third, they are able to communicate qualities of experience that cannot be expressed by the ordinary literal use of language. And fourth, they both evoke and serve to foster and clarify man's experience of an aspect of the world that can be called the "order of splendor" or the Divine. In describing this last function of religious symbols, Randall develops an aesthetic analogy.

The work of the painter, the musician, the poet, teaches us how to use our eyes, our ears, our minds, and our feelings with greater power and skill. . . . It shows us how to discern unsuspected qualities in the world encountered, latent powers and possibilities there resident. Still more, it makes us see the new qualities with which the world, in cooperation with the spirit of man, can clothe itself. . . . Is it otherwise with the prophet and the saint? They too can do something to us, they too can effect changes in us and in our world. . . . They teach us how to see what man's life in the world is, and what it might be. They teach us how to discern what human nature can make out of its natural conditions and materials. . . . They make us receptive to qualities of the world encountered; and they open our hearts to the new qualities with which that world, in cooperation with the spirit of man, can clothe itself. They enable us to see and feel the

16 Published in Boston by the Beacon Press, 1958.

17 Randall himself, in a paper published in 1954, in which he presented the same theory of religious language, said, "The position I am here trying to state I have been led to work out in connection with various courses on myths and symbols I have given jointly with Paul Tillich. . . . After long discussions, Mr. Tillich and I have found we are very close to agreement." *The Journal of Philosophy*, LI, No. 5 (March 4, 1954), 159. Tillich's article which develops his doctrine of symbols most clearly in the direction taken by Randall is "Religious Symbols and our Knowledge of God," *The Christian Scholar* (September, 1955).

18 Randall, *The Role of Knowledge in Western Religion* (Boston: Beacon Press, 1958), p. 114.

religious dimension of our world better, the "order of splendor," and of man's experience in and with it. They teach us how to find the Divine; they show us visions of God.[19]

It is to be noted that Randall's position represents a radical departure from the traditional assumptions of Western religion. For in speaking of "finding the Divine" and of being shown "visions of God," Randall does not mean to imply that God or the Divine exists as a reality independently of the human mind. He is speaking "symbolically." God is "...our ideals, our controlling values, our 'ultimate concern' ";[20] he is "...an intellectual symbol for the religious dimension of the world, for the Divine."[21] This religious dimension is "...a quality to be discriminated in human experience of the world, the splendor of the vision that sees beyond the actual into the perfected and eternal realm of the imagination."[22] This last statement, however, is enlivened by a philosophic rhetoric which may unintentionally obscure basic issues. The products of the human imagination are not eternal; they did not exist before man himself existed, and they can persist, even as imagined entities, only as long as men exist. The Divine, as defined by Randall, is the temporary mental construction or projection of a recently emerged animal inhabiting one of the satellites of a minor star. God is not, according to this view, the creator and the ultimate ruler of the universe; he is a fleeting ripple of imagination in a tiny corner of space-time.

Randall's theory of religion and of the function of religious language expresses with great clarity a way of thinking that in less clearly defined forms is widespread today and is, indeed, characteristic of our culture. This way of thinking is epitomized in the way in which the word "Religion" (or "faith" used virtually as a synonym) has largely come to replace the word "God." In contexts in which formerly questions were raised and debated concerning God, his existence, attributes, purpose, and deeds, the corresponding questions today typically concern Religion, its nature, function, forms, and pragmatic value. A shift has taken place from the term "God" as the head of a certain group of words and locutions to the term "Religion" as the new head of the same linguistic family.

There is, accordingly, much talk of Religion considered as an aspect of human culture. As Randall says, "Religion, we now see, is a distinctive human enterprise with a socially indispensable function of its own to perform."[23] In many universities and colleges there are departments devoted to studying the history and varieties of this phenomenon and the contribu-

---

19 Randall, *Knowledge in Western Religion,* pp. 128–29.
20 Ibid., p. 33.
21 Ibid., p. 112.
22 Ibid., p. 119.
23 Ibid., p. 6.

tion that it has brought to man's culture in general. Among the ideas treated in this connection, along with cult, priesthood, taboo, and many others, is the concept of God. For academic study, God is thus conceived as a subtopic within the larger subject of Religion.

At a more popular level Religion is widely regarded, in a psychological mode, as a human activity whose general function is to enable the individual to achieve harmony within himself and with his environment. One of the distinctive ways in which Religion fulfills this function is by preserving and promoting certain great ideas or symbols that possess the power to invigorate men's better aspirations. The most important and enduring of these symbols is God. Thus, at both academic and popular levels God is, in effect, defined in terms of Religion, as one of the concepts with which Religion works rather than Religion being defined in terms of God, as the field of men's varying responses to a real supernatural Being.

This displacement of "God" by "Religion" as the focus of a wide realm of discourse has brought with it a change in the character of the questions that are most persistently asked in this area. Concerning God, the traditional question has naturally been whether he exists or is real. But this is not a question that arises with regard to Religion. It is obvious that Religion exists; the important queries concern the purposes that it serves in human life, whether it ought to be cultivated, and if so, in what directions it may most profitably be developed. Under the pressure of these concerns, the question of the truth of religious beliefs has fallen into the background and the issue of their practical usefulness has come forward instead to occupy the center of attention.

In the perspective of history, is this pragmatic emphasis a surrogate for the older conception of objective religious realities, a substitute natural to an age of waning faith? Such a diagnosis is suggested by the observations of the agnostic, John Stuart Mill, in his famous essay on *The Utility of Religion.*

If religion, or any particular form of it, is true, its usefulness follows without other proof. If to know authentically in what order of things, under what government of the universe it is our destiny to live, were not useful, it is difficult to imagine what could be considered so. Whether a person is in a pleasant or in an unpleasant place, a palace or a prison, it cannot be otherwise than useful to him to know where he is. So long, therefore, as men accepted the teachings of their religion as positive facts, no more a matter of doubt than their own existence or the existence of the objects around them, to ask the use of believing it could not possibly occur to them. The utility of religion did not need to be asserted until the arguments for its truth had in a great measure ceased to convince. People must either have ceased to believe, or have ceased to rely on the belief of others, before they could take that inferior ground of defence without a consciousness of lowering what they were endeavouring to raise. An argument for the utility of religion is an appeal to unbelievers, to induce them to practice a well meant hypocrisy, or to semi-believers to make them avert their eyes from what might possibly shake their unstable belief, or finally to persons in general to abstain from expressing any doubts they may feel, since a fabric of immense importance to mankind is so insecure at its foundations that men must hold their breath in its neighbourhood for fear of blowing it down.[24]

Mill's words refer to mid-nineteenth-century England, which happens to have had much in common religiously with contemporary American society. One also recalls the critical remark of Bertrand Russell (likewise a nineteenth-century rationalist, although he happily lived on into the second half of the twentieth century), "I can respect the men who argue that religion is true and therefore ought to be believed, but I can feel only profound reprobation for those who say that religion ought to be believed because it is useful, and that to ask whether it is true is a waste of time."[25]

Comparing this current emphasis upon utility rather than truth with the thought of the great biblical exemplars of faith, we are at once struck by a startling reversal. There is a profound difference between serving and worshiping God and being "interested in Religion." God, if he is real, is our Creator. He is infinitely superior to ourselves, in worth as well as in power. He is One ". . . in whose eyes all hearts are open, all desires known, and from whom no secrets are hid." On the other hand, Religion stands before us as one of the various concerns that we may, at our own option, choose to pursue. In dealing with Religion and the religions, we occupy the appraiser's role; and God is subsumed within that which we appraise. There need be no bareing of one's life before divine judgment and mercy. We can deal instead with Religion, within which God is an idea, a concept whose history we can trace, and which we can analyze, define, and even revise. He is not, as in biblical thought, the living Lord of heaven and earth before whom men bow down in awe to worship and rise up with joy to serve.

The historical sources of the now prevalent and perhaps even dominant view of Religion as essentially an aspect of human culture are fairly evident. This view of Religion represents a logical development, within an increasingly technological society, of what has been variously called scientism, positivism, and naturalism. This development is based upon the assumption engendered by the tremendous, dramatic, and still accelerating growth of scientific knowledge and achievement that the truth concerning any aspect, or alleged aspect, of reality is to be found by the application of the methods of scientific investigation to the relevant phenomena. God is not a phenomenon available for scientific study, but Religion is. There can be a history, a phenomenology, a psychology, a sociology, and a comparative study of

[24] J. S. Mill, *Three Essays on Religion* (London: Longmans, Green & Co., 1875), pp. 69–70.
[25] Bertrand Russell, *Why I Am Not a Christian* (London: George Allen & Unwin Ltd., 1957), p. 172 (New York: Simon & Schuster, Inc., 1957), p. 197.

Religion. Hence, Religion has become an object of intensive investigation and God is perforce identified as an idea that occurs within this complex phenomenon of Religion.

ANOTHER NONCOGNITIVE ANALYSIS OF RELIGIOUS LANGUAGE

Another theory of the function of religion which, like Randall's, asserts the noncognitive character of religious language, has been offered by R. B. Braithwaite.[26] He suggests that religious assertions serve primarily an ethical function. The purpose of ethical statements is, according to Braithwaite, to express the speaker's adherence to a certain policy of action; they express ". . . the intention of the asserter to act in a particular sort of way specified in the assertion . . . when a man asserts that he ought to do so-and-so, he is using the assertion to declare that he resolves, to the best of his ability, to do so-and-so."[27] Thereby, of course, the speaker also recommends this way of behaving to others. Religious statements, likewise, express and recommend a commitment to a certain general policy or way of life. For example, a Christian's assertion that God is love (agape) is his indication of ". . . intention to follow an agapeistic way of life."[28]

Braithwaite next raises the question: when two religions (say Christianity and Buddhism) recommend essentially the same policy for living, in what sense are they *different religions?* There are, of course, wide divergences of ritual; but these, in Braithwaite's view, are relatively unimportant. The significant distinction lies in the different sets of stories (or myths or parables) that are associated in the two religions with adherence to their way of life.

It is not necessary, according to Braithwaite, that these stories be true or even that they be believed to be true. The connection between religious stories and the religious way of life is ". . . a psychological and causal one. It is an empirical psychological fact that many people find it easier to resolve upon and to carry through a course of action which is contrary to their natural inclinations if this policy is associated in their minds with

---

[26] R. B. Braithwaite, *An Empiricist's View of the Nature of Religious Belief* (Cambridge: Cambridge University Press, 1955). Reprinted in *The Existence of God*, ed. John Hick (New York: The Macmillan Company, 1964), and *Classical and Contemporary Readings in the Philosophy of Religion*, ed. J. Hick (Englewood Cliffs, N.J.: Prentice-Hall, Inc., 1970). Other philosophers who have independently developed noncognitive analyses of religious language which show a family resemblance to that of Braithwaite are Peter Munz, *Problems of Religious Knowledge* (London: Student Christian Movement Press Ltd., 1959); T. R. Miles, *Religion and the Scientific Outlook* (London: George Allen & Unwin Ltd., 1959); Paul F. Schmidt, *Religious Knowledge* (New York: The Free Press, 1961); and Paul Van Buren, *The Secular Meaning of the Gospel* (New York: The Macmillan Company, 1963).

[27] Braithwaite, *Nature of Religious Belief*, pp. 12–14.

[28] Ibid., p. 18.

certain stories. And in many people the psychological link is not appreciably weakened by the fact that the story associated with the behavior policy is not believed. Next to the Bible and the Prayer Book the most influential work in English Christian religious life has been a book whose stories are frankly recognized as fictitious—Bunyan's *Pilgrim's Progress*."[29]

In summary, Braithwaite states, "A religious assertion, for me, is the assertion of an intention to carry out a certain behavior policy, subsumable under a sufficiently general principle to be a moral one, together with the implicit or explicit statement, but not the assertion, of certain stories."[30]

Some questions may now be raised for discussion.

1. As in the case of Randall's theory, Braithwaite considers religious statements to function in a way that is different from the way they have, in fact, been used by the great majority of religious persons. In Braithwaite's form of Christianity, God has the status of a character in the associated fictional stories.

2. The ethical theory upon which Braithwaite bases his account of religious language holds that moral assertions are expressions of the asserter's intention to act in the way specified in his assertion. For example, "Lying is wrong" means "I intend never to lie." If this were so, it would follow that it would be logically impossible to *intend* to act wrongly. "Lying is wrong, but I intend to tell a lie" would be a sheer contradiction, equivalent to "I intend never to lie (= lying is wrong) but I intend to lie." This consequence conflicts with the way in which we actually speak in ethical contexts; sometimes people *do* knowingly intend to act wrongly.

3. The Christian stories to which Braithwaite refers in the course of his lecture are of very diverse logical types. They include straightforward historical statements about the life of Jesus, mythological expressions of belief in creation and a final judgment, and belief in the existence of God. Of these, only the first category appears to fit Braithwaite's own definition of a story as "...a proposition or set of propositions which are straightforwardly empirical propositions capable of empirical test."[31] Statements such as "God was in Christ reconciling the world to himself" or "God loves mankind" do not constitute stories in Braithwaite's sense. Thus, his category of religious stories takes account only of one relatively peripheral type of religious statement; it is unable to accommodate those central, more directly and distinctively religious statements that refer to God. To a great extent it is men's beliefs about God which impel them to an agapeistic way of life. Yet, these most important beliefs remain unanalyzed; for they cannot be placed in the only category that Braithwaite supplies, that of unproblematically factual beliefs.

[29] Ibid., p. 27.
[30] Ibid., p. 32.
[31] Ibid., p. 23.

4. Braithwaite holds that beliefs about God are relevant to a man's practical behavior because they provide it with psychological reinforcement. But another possible view of the matter is that the ethical significance of these beliefs consists in the way in which they render a certain way of life both attractive and rational. This view would seem to be consistent with the character of Jesus' ethical teaching. He did not demand that people live in a way that runs counter to their deepest desires and that would thus require some extraordinary counterbalancing inducement. Rather, he professed to reveal to them the true nature of the world in which they live, and in the light of this, to indicate the way in which their deepest desires might be fulfilled. In an important sense, then, Jesus did not propose any new motive for action. He did not set up a new end to be sought nor did he provide a new impulse toward an already familiar end. Instead, he offered a new vision or mode of apperception of the world, such that to live rationally in the world as thus seen is to live in the kind of way he described. He sought to replace the various attitudes and policies for living which express the sense of insecurity that is natural enough if the world really is an arena of competing interests in which each must safeguard himself and his own against the rival egoisms of his neighbors. If human life is essentially a form of animal life, and human civilization a refined jungle in which self-concern operates more subtly, but not less surely, than animal tooth and claw, then the quest for invulnerability in its many guises is entirely rational. To seek security in the form of power over others, whether physical, psychological, economic, or political, or in the form of recognition and acclaim, would then be indicated by the terms of the human situation. Jesus, however, rejected these attitudes and objectives as being based upon an estimate of the world that is false because it is atheistic; it assumes that there is no God, or at least none such as Jesus knew. Jesus was far from being an idealist if by this we mean one who sets up ideals unrelated to the facts and recommends that men be guided by them rather than by the realities of their lives. On the contrary, Jesus was a realist; he pointed to the life in which the neighbor is valued equally with the self as something indicated by the actual nature of the universe. He urged men to live in terms of reality. His morality differed from normal human practice because his view of reality differed from our normal view of the world. Whereas the ethic of egoism is ultimately atheistic, Jesus' ethic was radically and consistently theistic. It set forth the way of life that is appropriate when God, as Jesus depicted him, is wholeheartedly believed to be real. The pragmatic and in a sense prudential basis of Jesus' moral teaching is very clearly expressed in his parable of the two houses built on sand and on rock.[32] This parable claims

32 Matthew 7:24f.

that the universe is so constituted that to live in the way which Jesus has described is to build one's life upon enduring foundations, whereas to live in the opposite way is to go "against the grain" of things and to court ultimate disaster. The same thought occurs in the saying about the two ways, one of which leads to life and the other to destruction.[33] Jesus assumed that his hearers wanted to live in terms of reality and he was concerned with telling them the true nature of reality. From this point of view, the agapeistic way of life follows naturally, via the given structure of the human mind, from belief in the reality of God as *Agape*. However, belief in the reality, love, and power of God issues in the agapeistic way of life (like good fruit from a good tree)[34] only if that belief is taken literally and not merely symbolically. In order to render a distinctive style of life both attractive and rational, religious beliefs must be regarded as assertions of fact, not merely as imaginative fictions.

[33] Matthew 7:13–14.
[34] Matthew 7:16f.

CHAPTER SIX

The Problem
of Verification

THE QUESTION OF   In implicit opposition to all noncognitive accounts
VERIFIABILITY   of religious language, traditional Christian and Jewish
faith has always presumed the factual character of its
basic assertions. It is, of course, evident even to the most preliminary reflection that theological statements, having a unique subject matter, are not wholly like any other kind of statement. They constitute a special use of language, which it is the task of the philosophy of religion to examine. But the way in which this language operates within historic Judaism and Christianity is much closer to ordinary factual asserting than to either the expressing of aesthetic intuitions or the declaring of ethical policies.

In view of this deeply engrained tendency of traditional theism to use the language of fact, the development within contemporary philosophy of a criterion by which to distinguish the factual from the nonfactual is directly relevant to the study of religious language.

Prior to the philosophical movement that began in Vienna, Austria, after World War I and became known as Logical Positivism,[1] it was generally

---

[1] For a classic statement of the tenets of Logical Positivism, see A. J. Ayer, *Language, Truth, and Logic,* 2nd ed. (London: Victor Gollancz Ltd., 1946, and New York: Dover Publications, Inc., 1946).

assumed that in order to become accepted as true a proposition need only pass one test, a direct examination as to its truth or falsity. But the positivists instituted another qualifying examination that a proposition must pass before it can even compete for the Diploma of Truth. This previous examination is concerned with whether or not a proposition is meaningful. "Meaningful" in this context is a logical term; it is not a psychological term, as when we speak of "a very meaningful experience" or say of something that "it means a lot to me." To say that a proposition has meaning or, more strictly (as became evident in the discussions of the 1930's and 1940's), that it has factual or cognitive meaning, is to say that it is in principle verifiable, or at least "probabilifiable," by reference to human experience. This means, in effect, that its truth or falsity must make some possible experienceable difference. If its truth or falsity makes no difference that could possibly be observed, the proposition is cognitively meaningless; it does not embody a factual assertion.

Suppose, for example, the startling news is announced one morning that overnight the entire physical universe has instantaneously doubled in size and that the speed of light has doubled. At first, this news seems to point to a momentous scientific discovery. All the items composing the universe, including our own bodies, are now twice as big as they were yesterday. But the inevitable questions concerning the evidence for this report must be raised. How can anyone know that the universe has doubled in size? What observable difference does it make whether this is so or not; what events or appearances are supposed to reveal it? On further reflection, it becomes clear that there *could not* be any evidence for this particular proposition. For if the entire universe has doubled and the speed of light has doubled with it, our measurements have also doubled and we can never know that any change had taken place. If our measuring rod has expanded with the objects to be measured, it cannot measure their expansion. In order adequately to acknowledge the systematic impossibility of testing such a proposition as that about the size of the universe, it seems best to classify it as (cognitively) meaningless. It first seems to be a genuinely factual assertion, but under scrutiny it proves to lack the basic characteristic of an assertion, namely, that it must make an experienceable difference whether the facts are as alleged or not.

For another example, consider the famous rabbit which at one time haunted philosophical discussions in Oxford. It is a very special rabbit—invisible, intangible, inaudible, weightless, and odorless. When the rabbit has been defined by all these negations, does it still make sense to insist that such a creature exists? It is difficult to avoid a negative answer. It seems clear that when every experienceable feature has been removed, there is nothing left about which we can make assertions.

The basic principle—representing a modified version of the original

Verifiability Principle of the logical positivists—that a factual assertion is one whose truth or falsity makes some experienceable difference, has been applied to theological propositions. John Wisdom opened this recent chapter in the philosophy of religion with his now famous parable of the gardener, which deserves to be quoted here in full.

Two people return to their long-neglected garden and find among the weeds a few of the old plants surprisingly vigorous. One says to the other "It must be that a gardener has been coming and doing something about these plants." Upon inquiry they find that no neighbor has ever seen anyone at work in their garden. The first man says to the other "He must have worked while people slept." The other says, "No, someone would have heard him and besides, anybody who cared about the plants would have kept down these weeds." The first man says, "Look at the way these are arranged. There is purpose and a feeling for beauty here. I believe that someone comes, someone invisible to mortal eyes. I believe that the more carefully we look the more we shall find confirmation of this." They examine the garden ever so carefully and sometimes they come on new things suggesting that a gardener comes and sometimes they come on new things suggesting the contrary and even that a malicious person has been at work. Besides examining the garden carefully they also study what happens to gardens left without attention. Each learns all the other learns about this and about the garden. Consequently, when after all this, one says "I still believe a gardener comes" while the other says "I don't" their different words now reflect no difference as to what they have found in the garden, no difference as to what they would find in the garden if they looked further and no difference about how fast untended gardens fall into disorder. At this stage, in this context, the gardener hypothesis has ceased to be experimental, the difference between one who accepts and one who rejects it is not now a matter of the one expecting something the other does not expect. What is the difference between them? The one says, "A gardener comes unseen and unheard. He is manifested only in his works with which we are all familiar," the other says "There is no gardener" and with this difference in what they say about the gardener goes a difference in how they feel towards the garden, in spite of the fact that neither expects anything of it which the other does not expect.[2]

Wisdom is here suggesting that the theist and the atheist do not disagree about the empirical (experienceable) facts, or about any observations which they anticipate in the future; they are, instead, reacting in different ways to the same set of facts. They are not making mutually contradicting assertions but are rather expressing different feelings. Understanding them in this way, we can no longer say in any usual sense that one is right and the other wrong. They both really feel about the world in the ways that

[2] "Gods,," first published in *Proceedings of the Aristotelian Society* (London, 1944–1945); reprinted here by permission of the editor. Reprinted in *Logic and Language*, I, ed. Antony Flew (Oxford: Basil Blackwell, and New York: Mott Ltd., 1951); in John Wisdom, *Philosophy and Psychoanalysis* (Oxford: Basil Blackwell, and New York: Mott Ltd., 1953), pp. 154–55; and in John Hick, ed., *Classical and Contemporary Readings in the Philosophy of Religion* (Englewood Cliffs, N.J.: Prentice-Hall, Inc., 2nd ed., 1970).

their words indicate. But expressions of feelings do not constitute assertions about the world. We would have to speak, instead, of these different feelings being more or less satisfying or valuable: as Santayana said, religions are not true or false but better or worse. According to Wisdom there is no disagreement about the experienceable facts, the settlement of which would determine whether the theist or the atheist is right. In other words, neither of the rival positions is, even in principle, verifiable.

The more recent phase of the debate has shifted from the idea of verifiability to the complementary idea of falsifiability. The question has been posed whether there is any conceivable event which, if it were to occur, would decisively refute theism? Are there any possible developments of our experience with which theism would be incompatible; or is it equally compatible with whatever may happen? Is anything ruled out by belief in God? Anthony Flew, who has presented the challenge in terms of the Judaic-Christian belief in a loving God, writes as follows:

> Now it often seems to people who are not religious as if there was no conceivable event or series of events the occurrence of which would be admitted by sophisticated religious people to be a sufficient reason for conceding "There wasn't a God after all" or "God does not really love us then." Someone tells us that God loves us as a father loves his children. We are reassured. But then we see a child dying of inoperable cancer of the throat. His earthly father is driven frantic in his efforts to help, but his Heavenly Father reveals no obvious sign of concern. Some qualification is made—God's love is "not a merely human love" or it is "an inscrutable love," perhaps—and we realize that such sufferings are quite compatible with the truth of the assertion that "God loves us as a father (but, of course...)." We are reassured again. But then perhaps we ask: what is this assurance of God's (appropriately qualified) love worth, what is this apparent guarantee really a guarantee against? Just what would have to happen not merely (morally and wrongly) to tempt but also (logically and rightly) to entitle us to say "God does not love us" or even "God does not exist"? I therefore put... the simple central questions, "What would have to occur or to have occurred to constitute for you a disproof of the love of, or of the existence of, God?"[3]

TWO SUGGESTED SOLUTIONS   In response to the challenge thus formulated by Flew, R. M. Hare has introduced the notion of *bliks*.

Hare concedes that it is the nature of religious beliefs to be held in such a way that nothing could ever count decisively against them, and that they cannot, therefore, be properly classified as assertions that might be true or false. What, then, are they? Coining a word, he suggests that they express a distinctive *blik,* a *blik* being an unverifiable and unfalsifiable

3 Flew in *New Essays in Philosophical Theology* (London: S.C.M. Press Ltd. 1955, and New York: The Macmillan Company, 1956), pp. 98–99. The *New Essays* discussion by Flew, Hare, Mitchell, and Crombie is reprinted in Hick, ed., *Classical and Contemporary Readings in the Philosophy of Religion.*

interpretation of one's experience. Suppose, for example, a lunatic is convinced that all the professors in a certain college are intent upon murdering him. It will be vain to try to allay his suspicions by introducing him to a series of kindly and inoffensive professors, for he will only see a particularly devious cunning in their apparently friendly manner. He does not hold his belief in a way that is open to confirmation or refutation by experience; he has a *blik*. He has an insane *blik* about the professors, and the rest of us have a sane *blik* about them. "It is [says Hare] important to realize that we have a sane one, not no *blik* at all; for there must be two sides to any argument—if he has a wrong *blik,* then those who are right about dons must have a right one. Flew has shown that a *blik* does not consist in an assertion or system of them; but nevertheless it is very important to have the right *blik*."[4]

Other instances which Hare offers of sane *bliks* are confidence in the rigidity of the steel in one's car; the assumption that the physical world has a stable character so that, for example, objects will not suddenly appear or disappear or be transformed into something else; and the belief that events occur within a causal system and not at random.

Suppose we believe that everything that happened, happened by pure chance. This would not of course be an assertion; for it is compatible with anything happening or not happening, and so, incidentally, is its contradictory. But if we had this belief, we should not be able to explain or predict or plan anything. Thus, although we should not be *asserting* anything different from those of a more normal belief, there would be a great difference between us; and this is the sort of difference that there is between those who really believe in God and those who really disbelieve in him.[5]

Hare's notion of the *blik* has been legitimately criticized as failing to separate cases that are too diverse to be properly lumped together.[6] The basic difficulty, however, is that Hare's suggestion, considered as an answer to Flew, does not answer Flew and, indeed, does not profess to. Hare abandons as indefensible the traditional view of religious statements as being or entailing assertions that are true or false. Probably everyone would agree that, when sincerely held, religious beliefs make an important difference *to the believer*. They affect the ways he feels, talks, and acts—as does the lunatic's *blik* about the professors. But a serious and rational concern with religion will inevitably make us want to know whether the way the believer feels and acts is appropriate to the actual character of the universe, and whether the things he says as a believer are true. We want to distinguish, in Hare's terminology, between right and wrong *bliks*. In the previously quoted passage, Hare assumes that one can make this distinction;

[4] Hare in *New Essays in Philosophical Theology,* p. 100.
[5] Ibid., pp. 101–2.
[6] H. J. N. Horsburgh, "Mr. Hare on Theology and Falsification," *The Philosophical Quarterly,* 6, No. 24 (July, 1956).

for he identifies one *blik* as sane and the contrary *blik* as insane. But there seems to be an inconsistency in his position here, for a discrimination between sane (= right) and insane (= wrong) *bliks* is ruled out by his insistence that *bliks* are unverifiable and unfalsifiable. If experience can never yield either confirmation or disconfirmation of religious *bliks,* there is no basis for speaking of them as being right or wrong, appropriate or inappropriate, sane or insane. These distinctions make sense only if it also makes sense to refer to tests, evidence, and verification. It is precisely this confirmation that Flew has demanded in relation to religious beliefs. It seems, then, that Hare has neither met Flew's challenge nor shown a way of avoiding it.

Another Oxford philosopher, Basil Mitchell, in his response to Flew, took an opposite line from that of Hare and sought to show that religious beliefs are genuinely factual in character even though they are not straight-forwardly verifiable or falsifiable. Mitchell recounts his own parable. A member of the resistance movement in an occupied country meets a stranger who deeply impresses him as being truthful and trustworthy, and who claims to be the resistance leader. He urges the partisan to have faith in him whatever may happen. Sometimes the stranger is seen apparently aiding the resistance and sometimes apparently collaborating with the enemy. But the partisan continues in trust. He admits that on the face of it some of the stranger's actions strain this trust. However he has faith, even though at times his faith is sorely tried, that there is a satisfactory explanation of the stranger's ambiguous behavior. "It is here [says Mitchell] that my parable differs from Hare's. The partisan admits that many things may and do count against his belief: whereas Hare's lunatic who has a *blik* about dons doesn't admit that anything counts against his *blik*. Nothing *can* count against *bliks*. Also the partisan has a reason for having in the first instance committed himself, viz. the character of the Stranger; whereas the lunatic has no reason for his *blik* about dons—because, of course, you can't have reasons for *bliks*."[7]

Mitchell's parable is concerned with a straightforward matter of fact which can, in principle, be definitely ascertained. The stranger himself knows on which side he is; and after the war, when all the facts are brought to light, the ambiguity of his behavior will be resolved and his true character made clear. Thus, Mitchell is concerned with stressing the similarity rather than the dissimilarity between religious beliefs and ordinary, unproblematic factual beliefs.[8] The idea of eschatological verification,

---

[7] Mitchell in *New Essays in Philosophical Theology,* p. 105.

[8] Flew's reply to Mitchell's suggestion was to underline the difference between the stranger in the parable and the supposed case of God. If God is omnipotent, omniscient, and all good, why should there be any ambiguity and any room for doubt as to his goodness? This is the ancient problem of evil, which has been discussed to some extent in Chapter 3.

to be introduced in the next section, can be seen as continuing the same line of thought.

THE IDEA OF
ESCHATOLOGICAL
VERIFICATION

I should like now to offer for the reader's consideration a constructive suggestion based upon the fact that Christianity includes afterlife beliefs.[9] Here are some preliminary points.

1. The verification of a factual assertion is not the same as a logical demonstration of it. The central core of the idea of verification is the removal of grounds for rational doubt. That a proposition, p, is verified means that something happens which makes it clear that p is true. A question is settled, so that there is no longer room for rational doubt concerning it. The way in which such grounds are excluded varies of course with the subject matter. But the common feature in all cases of verification is the ascertaining of truth by the removal of grounds for rational doubt. Whenever such grounds have been removed, we rightly speak of verification having taken place.

2. Sometimes it is necessary to put oneself in a certain position or to perform some particular operation as a prerequisite of verification. For example, one can only verify "There is a table in the next room" by going into the next room; but it is to be noted that no one is compelled to do this.

3. Therefore, although "verifiable" normally means "publicly verifiable" (i.e., capable in principle of being verified by anyone) it does not follow that a given verifiable proposition has in fact been or will in fact ever be verified by everyone. The number of people who verify a particular true proposition depends upon all manner of contingent factors.

4. It is possible for a proposition to be in principle verifiable but not in principle falsifiable. Consider, for example, the proposition that "there are three successive sevens in the decimal determination of π." So far as the value of π has been worked out, it does not contain a series of three sevens; but since the operation can proceed *ad infinitum* it will always be true that a triple seven may occur at a point not yet reached in anyone's calculations. Accordingly, the proposition may one day be verified if it is true but can never be falsified if it is false.

[9] This suggestion is presented more fully in John Hick, "Theology and Verification," *Theology Today,* XVII, No. 1 (April, 1960), reprinted in *The Existence of God,* John Hick, ed. (New York: The Macmillan Company, 1964) and developed in *Faith and Knowledge,* 2nd ed. (Ithaca, N.Y.: Cornell University Press, 1966, and London: Macmillan & Company Ltd., 1967), Chap. 8. It is criticized by Paul F. Schmidt in *Religious Knowledge* (New York: The Free Press, 1961), pp. 58–60; by William Blackstone, *The Problem of Religious Knowledge* (Englewood Cliffs, N.J.: Prentice-Hall, Inc., 1963), pp. 112–16; and by Kai Nielsen, "Eschatological Verification," *Canadian Journal of Theology,* IX, No. 4 (October, 1963), and *Contemporary Critiques of Religion* (London: Macmillan & Company Ltd. and New York: Herder & Herder, Inc., 1971), Chap. 4.

5. The hypothesis of continued conscious existence after bodily death provides another instance of a proposition that is verifiable if true but not falsifiable if false. This hypothesis entails a prediction that one will, after the date of one's bodily death, have conscious experiences, including the experience of remembering that death. This is a prediction that will be verified in one's own experience if it is true but that cannot be falsified if it is false. That is to say, it can be false, but *that* it is false can never be a fact that anyone has experientially verified. This principle does not undermine the meaningfulness of the survival hypothesis, for if its prediction is true, it will be known to be true.

The idea of eschatological verification can now be indicated—following the example of other writers on this problem—in yet another parable.[10]

Two men are travelling together along a road. One of them believes that it leads to the Celestial City, the other that it leads nowhere; but since this is the only road there is, both must travel it. Neither has been this way before; therefore, neither is able to say what they will find around each corner. During their journey they meet with moments of refreshment and delight, and with moments of hardship and danger. All the time one of them thinks of his journey as a pilgrimage to the Celestial City. He interprets the pleasant parts as encouragements and the obstacles as trials of his purpose and lessons in endurance, prepared by the king of that city and designed to make of him a worthy citizen of the place when at last he arrives. The other, however, believes none of this, and sees their journey as an unavoidable and aimless ramble. Since he has no choice in the matter, he enjoys the good and endures the bad. For him there is no Celestial City to be reached, no all-encompassing purpose ordaining their journey; there is only the road itself and the luck of the road in good weather and in bad.

During the course of the journey, the issue between them is not an experimental one. They do not entertain different expectations about the coming details of the road, but only about its ultimate destination. Yet, when they turn the last corner, it will be apparent that one of them has been right all the time and the other wrong. Thus, although the issue between them has not been experimental, it has nevertheless been a real issue. They have not merely felt differently about the road, for one was feeling appropriately and the other inappropriately in relation to the actual state of affairs. Their opposed interpretations of the situation have constituted genuinely rival assertions, whose assertion-status has the peculiar characteristic of being guaranteed retrospectively by a future crux.

This parable, like all parables, has narrow limitations. It is designed to make only one point: that Judaic-Christian theism postulates an ultimate

[10] This "parable" is reprinted, by permission of the Cornell University Press, from the first edition of my *Faith and Knowledge*, pp. 150–52.

unambiguous existence *in patria,* as well as our present ambiguous existence *in via.* There is a state of having arrived as well as a state of journeying, an eternal heavenly life as well as an earthly pilgrimage. The alleged future experience cannot, of course, be appealed to as evidence for theism as a present interpretation of our experience; but it does suffice to render the choice between theism and atheism a real and not merely an empty or verbal choice.

The universe as envisaged by the theist, then, differs as a totality from the universe as envisaged by the atheist. However, from our present standpoint within the universe, this difference does not involve a difference in the objective content of each or even any of its passing moments. The theist and the atheist do not (or need not) expect different events to occur in the successive details of the temporal process. They do not (or need not) entertain divergent expectations of the course of history viewed from within. However, the theist does and the atheist does not expect that when history is completed it will be seen to have led to a particular end state and to have fulfilled a specific purpose, namely, that of creating "children of God."

SOME DIFFICULTIES AND COMPLICATIONS

Even if it were granted (as many philosophers would not be willing to grant) that it makes sense to speak of continued personal existence after death, this can not by itself render belief in God verifiable. Nor would an actual experience of survival necessarily serve to verify theism. It might be taken as just a surprising natural fact. The atheist, able to remember his life on earth, might find that the universe has turned out to be more complex, and perhaps more to be approved of, than he had realized. But the mere fact of survival, with a new body in a new environment, would not demonstrate to him the reality of God. The life to come might turn out to be as religiously ambiguous as this present life. It might still be quite unclear whether or not there is a God.

Should appeal be made at this point to the traditional doctrine, which figures especially in Catholic and mystical theology, of the Beatific Vision of God? The difficulty is to attach any precise meaning to this phrase.[11] If it is to be more than a metaphor for one knows not what, it signifies that embodied beings see (visually, not metaphorically) the visible figure of the deity. But to speak in this way is apparently to think of God as a finite object in space. If we are to follow the implications of the deeper insights of the Western theological tradition, we shall have to think of an experienced situation that points unambiguously to the reality of God,

[11] Aquinas attempts to make the idea intelligible in his *Summa contra Gentiles,* Book III, Chap. 51.

rather than of a literal vision of the deity. The consciousness of God will still be, formally, a matter of faith in that it will continue to involve an activity of interpretation. But the data to be interpreted, instead of being bafflingly ambiguous, will at all points confirm religious faith. We are thus postulating a situation that contrasts in an important respect with our present situation. Our present experience of this world in some ways seems to support and in other ways to contradict a religious faith. Some events suggest the reality of an unseen and benevolent intelligence, and others suggest that no such intelligence can be at work. Our environment is thus religiously ambiguous. In order for us to be aware of this fact, we must already have some idea, however vague, of what it would be for a world to be not ambiguous but on the contrary wholly evidential of God. Is it possible to draw out this presupposed idea of a religiously unambiguous situation?

Although it is difficult to say what future experiences would verify theism in general, it is less difficult to say what would verify the more specific claims of such a religion as Christianity, with its own built-in eschatological beliefs. The system of ideas that surrounds the Christian concept of God, and in the light of which that concept has to be understood, includes expectations concerning the final fulfillment of God's purpose for mankind in the "Kingdom of God." The experience that would verify Christian belief in God is the experience of participating in that eventual fulfillment. According to the New Testament, the general nature of God's purpose for human life is the creation of "children of God" who shall participate in eternal life. One can say this much without professing advance knowledge of the concrete forms of such a fulfillment. The situation is analogous to that of a small child looking forward to adult life and then, having grown to adulthood, looking back upon childhood. The child possesses and can use correctly the concept of "being grown up," although he does not yet know exactly what it is like to be grown up. When he reaches adulthood he is, nevertheless, able to know that he has reached it. For his understanding of adult maturity grows as he himself matures. Something analogous may be supposed to happen in the case of the fulfillment of the divine purpose for human life. That fulfillment may be as far removed from our present condition as is mature adulthood from the mind of a little child. Indeed, it may be much further removed; but we already possess some notion of it (given in the person of Christ) and as we move toward it our concept will, thereby, become more adequate. If and when we finally reach that fulfillment, the problem of recognizing it will have disappeared in the process.

A further feature is added by specifically Christian theism. The New Testament expresses this in visual symbols when it says that the Lamb will be in the midst of the throne of the Kingdom. That is to say, in the situation in which the divine purpose for man is fulfilled, the person of Christ will be manifestly exalted. This element completes the circle of verification, linking the future fulfillment situation directly with that which is to be verified, namely, the authority of the Christ who is the source and basis of Christian faith.

It is this aspect of Christian prediction that makes it possible to meet indirectly the more basic problem of recognition in the awareness of God. A number of philosophers have pointed out the logical difficulty involved in any claim to have encountered God.[12] How could one know that it was *God* whom one had encountered? God is described in Christian theology in terms of various absolute qualities, such as omnipotence, omnipresence, perfect goodness, and infinite love. Such absolute qualities cannot be observed by us, as can their finite analogues, limited power, local presence, finite goodness, and human love. One can recognize that a being whom one encounters has a given finite degree of power, but how does one recognize that he has unlimited power? How does one perceive that his goodness and love, although appearing to exceed any human goodness and love, are actually infinite? Such qualities cannot be given in human experience. One might claim to have encountered a Being whom one presumes, or trusts, or hopes to be God; but one cannot claim to have encountered a Being whom one *recognized* to be the infinite, almighty, eternal Creator.

In Christianity, God is known as "the God and Father of our Lord Jesus Christ." He is defined as the Being about whom Jesus taught; the Being in relation to whom he lived, and into a relationship with whom he brought his disciples; the Being whose *agape* toward men was seen on earth in the life of Jesus. In short, God is the transcendent Creator who is held to have revealed himself in Christ. Jesus' teaching about the Father is accordingly accepted as a part of that self-disclosure, and it is from this teaching (together with that of the prophets who preceded him) that Christianity professes to derive its knowledge of God's transcendent being. Only God himself can know his own infinite nature; and our human belief about that nature is based, according to Christianity, upon his self-revelation to men in Christ. Such beliefs about God's infinite being are not capable of observational verification, being beyond the scope of human experience, but they may be susceptible to indirect verification by the exclusion of rational doubt concerning the authority of Christ. An experience of the reign of the Son in the Kingdom of the Father would confirm that authority, and therewith, by extension, the validity of Jesus' teaching concerning the character of God in his infinite transcendent nature.

[12] For example, Ronald Hepburn, *Christianity and Paradox* (London: C. A. Watts & Company Ltd., 1958), pp. 56f.

Even an experience of the realization of the promised Kingdom of God, with Christ reigning as Lord of the New Age, could not constitute a logical certification of his claims, nor of a belief in God founded upon those claims. However, it is a basic position of empiricist philosophy that matters of fact are not susceptible of logical proof. The most that can be desired is such weight of evidence as leaves no room for rational doubt; and it might well be claimed on behalf of Christianity that the eschatological verification implied in Christian theology would constitute such evidence.

"EXISTS," "FACT,"   Can we, then, properly ask whether God "exists"?
AND "REAL"   If we do so, what precisely are we asking? Does
                                 "exist" have a single meaning, so that one can ask, in the same sense, "Do flying fish exist; does the square root of minus one exist; does the Freudian superego exist; does God exist?" It seems clear that we are asking very different kinds of questions in these cases. To ask whether flying fish exist is to ask whether a certain form of organic life is to be found in the oceans of the world. On the other hand, to ask whether the square root of minus one exists is not to ask whether there is a certain kind of material object somewhere, but is to pose a question about the conventions of mathematics. To ask whether the superego exists is to ask whether one accepts the Freudian picture of the structure of the psyche; and this is a decision to which a great variety of considerations may be relevant. To ask whether God exists is to ask—what? Not, certainly, whether there is a particular physical object. Is it (as in the mathematical case) to enquire about linguistic conventions? Or is it (as in the psychological case) to enquire about a great mass of varied considerations— perhaps even the character of our experience as a whole? What, in short, does it mean to affirm that God exists?

It would be no answer to this question to refer to the idea of divine aseity[13] and to say that the difference between the ways in which God and other realities exist is that God exists necessarily and everything else contingently. For we still want to know what it is that God is doing or undergoing in existing necessarily rather than contingently. (We do not learn what electricity is by being told that some electrical circuits have an alternating and others a direct current; likewise, we do not learn what it is to exist by being told that some things exist necessarily and others contingently.)

For those who adopt one or another of the various noncognitive accounts of religious language, there is no problem concerning the sense in which God "exists." If they use the expression "God exists" at all, they under-

13 For an explanation of this term, see p. 7.

stand it as referring obliquely to the speaker's own feelings or attitudes or moral commitments, or to the character of the empirical world. But what account of "God exists" can be given by the traditional theist, who holds that God exists as the Creator and the ultimate Ruler of the universe?

The same question can be posed in terms of the idea of "fact." The theist claims that the existence of God is a question of fact, rather than merely of definition or of linguistic usage. The theist also uses the term "real," and claims that God is real or a reality. But what do these words mean in this context? The problem is essentially the same whether one employs "exist," "fact," or "real."

This is a question on the growing edge of the philosophy of religion, and one to which theistic thinkers will have to devote further attention if their position is to be philosophically intelligible.

Without attempting to solve the problem here, it may be suggested that the common core to the concepts of "existence," "fact," and "reality" is the idea of "making a difference." To say that x exists or is real, that it is a fact that there is an x, is to claim that the character of the universe differs in some specific way from the character that an x-less universe would have. The nature of this difference will naturally depend upon the character of the x in question. And the meaning of "God exists" will be indicated by spelling out the past, present, and future difference which God's existence is alleged to make within human experience.

CHAPTER SEVEN

Human Destiny: Immortality and Resurrection

THE IMMORTALITY OF THE SOUL   Some kind of distinction between physical body and immaterial or semimaterial soul seems to be as old as human culture; the existence of such a distinction has been indicated by the manner of burial of the earliest human skeletons yet discovered. Anthropologists offer various conjectures about the origin of the distinction: perhaps it was first suggested by memories of dead persons; by dreams of them; by the sight of reflections of oneself in water and on other bright surfaces; or by meditation upon the significance of religious rites which grew up spontaneously in face of the fact of death.

It was Plato (428/7–348/7 B.C.), the philosopher who has most deeply and lastingly influenced Western culture, who systematically developed the body–mind dichotomy and first attempted to prove the immortality of the soul.[1]

Plato argues that although the body belongs to the sensible world,[2] and shares its changing and impermanent nature, the intellect is related to the unchanging realities of which we are aware when we think not of particular

---

[1] *Phaedo.*
[2] The world known to us through our physical senses.

good things but of Goodness itself, not of specific just acts but of Justice itself, and of the other "universals" or eternal Ideas in virtue of which physical things and events have their own specific characteristics. Being related to this higher and abiding realm, rather than to the evanescent world of sense, reason or the soul is immortal. Hence, one who devotes his life to the contemplation of eternal realities rather than to the gratification of the fleeting desires of the body will find at death that whereas his body turns to dust, his soul gravitates to the realm of the unchanging, there to live forever. Plato painted an awe-inspiring picture, of haunting beauty and persuasiveness, which has moved and elevated the minds of men in many different centuries and lands. Nevertheless, it is not today (as it was during the first centuries of the Christian era) the common philosophy of the West; and a demonstration of immortality which presupposes Plato's metaphysical system cannot claim to constitute a proof for the twentieth-century disbeliever.

Plato used the further argument that the only things that can suffer destruction are those that are composite, since to destroy something means to disintegrate it into its constituent parts. All material bodies are composite; the soul, however, is simple and therefore imperishable. This argument was adopted by Aquinas and has become standard in Roman Catholic theology, as in the following passage from the modern Catholic philosopher, Jacques Maritain:

A spiritual soul cannot be corrupted, since it possesses no matter; it cannot be disintegrated, since it has no substantial parts; it cannot lose its individual unity, since it is self-subsisting, nor its internal energy, since it contains within itself all the sources of its energies. The human soul cannot die. Once it exists, it cannot disappear; it will necessarily exist for ever, endure without end. Thus, philosophic reason, put to work by a great metaphysician like Thomas Aquinas, is able to prove the immortality of the human soul in a demonstrative manner.[3]

This type of reasoning has been criticized on several grounds. Kant pointed out that although it is true that a simple substance cannot disintegrate, consciousness may nevertheless cease to exist through the diminution of its intensity to zero.[4] Modern psychology has also questioned the basic premise that the mind is a simple entity. It seems instead to be a structure of only relative unity, normally fairly stable and tightly integrated but capable under stress of various degrees of division and dissolution. This comment from psychology makes it clear that the assumption that the soul is a simple substance is not an empirical observation but a metaphysical theory. As such, it cannot provide the basis for a general proof of immortality.

[3] Jacques Maritain, *The Range of Reason* (London: Geoffrey Bles Ltd. and New York: Charles Scribner's Sons, 1953), p. 60.
[4] Kant, *Critique of Pure Reason, Transcendental Dialectic,* "Refutation of Mendelessohn's Proof of the Permanence of the Soul."

The body–soul distinction, first formulated as a philosophical doctrine in ancient Greece, was baptized into Christianity, ran through the medieval period, and entered the modern world with the public status of a self-evident truth when it was redefined in the seventeenth century by Descartes. Since World War II, however, the Cartesian mind–matter dualism, having been taken for granted for many centuries, has been strongly criticized by philosophers of the contemporary analytical school.[5] It is argued that the words that describe mental characteristics and operations—such as "intelligent," "thoughtful," "carefree," "happy," "calculating" and the like—apply in practice to types of human behavior and to behavioral dispositions. They refer to the empirical individual, the observable human being who is born and grows and acts and feels and dies, and not to the shadowy proceedings of a mysterious "ghost in the machine." Man is thus very much what he appears to be—a creature of flesh and blood, who behaves and is capable of behaving in a characteristic range of ways—rather than a nonphysical soul incomprehensibly interacting with a physical body.

As a result of this development much mid-twentieth-century philosophy has come to see man in the way he is seen in the biblical writings, not as an eternal soul temporarily attached to a mortal body, but as a form of finite, mortal, psychophysical life. Thus, the Old Testament scholar, J. Pedersen, says of the Hebrews that for them "...the body is the soul in its outward form."[6] This way of thinking has led to quite a different conception of death from that found in Plato and the neo-Platonic strand in European thought.

THE RE-CREATION OF THE PSYCHO-PHYSICAL PERSON

Only toward the end of the Old Testament period did after-life beliefs come to have any real importance in Judaism. Previously, Hebrew religious insight had focused so fully upon God's covenant with the nation, as an organism that continued through the centuries while successive generations lived and died, that the thought of a divine purpose for the individual, a purpose that transcended this present life, developed only when the breakdown of the nation as a political entity threw into prominence the individual and the problem of his personal destiny.

When a positive conviction arose of God's purpose holding the individual in being beyond the crisis of death, this conviction took the non-Platonic form of belief in the resurrection of the body. By the turn of the eras, this had become an article of faith for one Jewish sect, the Pharisees, although it was still rejected as an innovation by the more conservative Sadducees.

[5] Gilbert Ryle's *The Concept of Mind* (London: Hutchinson & Co., Ltd., 1949) is a classic statement of this critique.

[6] *Israel* (London: Oxford University Press, 1926), I, 170.

The religious difference between the Platonic belief in the immortality of the soul, and the Judaic-Christian belief in the resurrection of the body is that the latter postulates a special divine act of re-creation. This produces a sense of utter dependence upon God in the hour of death, a feeling that is in accordance with the biblical understanding of man as having been formed out of "the dust of the earth,"[7] a product (as we say today) of the slow evolution of life from its lowly beginnings in the primeval slime. Hence, in the Jewish and Christian conception, death is something real and fearful. It is not thought to be like walking from one room to another, or taking off an old coat and putting on a new one. It means sheer unqualified extinction—passing out from the lighted circle of life into "death's dateless night." Only through the sovereign creative love of God can there be a new existence beyond the grave.

What does "the resurrection of the dead" mean? Saint Paul's discussion provides the basic Christian answer to this question.[8] His conception of the general resurrection (distinguished from the unique resurrection of Jesus) has nothing to do with the resuscitation of corpses in a cemetery. It concerns God's re-creation or reconstitution of the human psychophysical individual, not as the organism that has died but as a *soma pneumatikon,* a "spiritual body," inhabiting a spiritual world as the physical body inhabits our present physical world.

A major problem confronting any such doctrine is that of providing criteria of personal identity to link the earthly life and the resurrection life. Paul does not specifically consider this question, but one may, perhaps, develop his thought along lines such as the following.[9]

Suppose, first, that someone—John Smith—living in the USA were suddenly and inexplicably to disappear from before the eyes of his friends, and that at the same moment an exact replica of him were inexplicably to appear in India. The person who appears in India is exactly similar in both physical and mental characteristics to the person who disappeared in America. There is continuity of memory, complete similarity of bodily features including fingerprints, hair and eye coloration, and stomach contents, and also of beliefs, habits, emotions, and mental dispositions. Further, the "John Smith" replica thinks of himself as being the John Smith who disappeared in the USA. After all possible tests have been made and have proved positive, the factors leading his friends to accept "John Smith" as John Smith would surely prevail and would cause them to overlook even his mysterious transference from one continent to another, rather than

---

[7] Genesis, 2:7; Psalm 103:14.

[8] I Corinthians 15.

[9] The following paragraphs are adapted, with permission, from a section of my article, "Theology and Verification," published in *Theology Today* (April, 1960) and reprinted in *The Existence of God* (New York: The Macmillan Company, 1964).

treat "John Smith," with all John Smith's memories and other characteristics, as someone other than John Smith.

Suppose, second, that our John Smith, instead of inexplicably disappear-
ing, dies, but that at the moment of his death a "John Smith" replica,
again complete with memories and all other characteristics, appears in
India. Even with the corpse on our hands we would, I think, still have
to accept this "John Smith" as the John Smith who died. We would have
to say that he had been miraculously re-created in another place.

Now suppose, third, that on John Smith's death the "John Smith" replica
appears, not in India, but as a resurrection replica in a different world
altogether, a resurrection world inhabited only by resurrected persons. This
world occupies its own space distinct from that with which we are now
familiar. That is to say, an object in the resurrection world is not situated
at any distance or in any direction from the objects in our present world,
although each object in either world is spatially related to every other
object in the same world.

This supposition provides a model by which one may conceive of the
divine re-creation of the embodied human personality. In this model, the
element of the strange and the mysterious has been reduced to a minimum
by following the view of some of the early Church Fathers that the resurrection body has the same shape as the physical body,[10] and ignoring Paul's
own hint that it may be as unlike the physical body as a full grain of
wheat differs from the wheat seed.[11]

What is the basis for this Judaic-Christian belief in the divine re-creation
or reconstitution of the human personality after death? There is, of course,
an argument from authority, in that life after death is taught throughout
the New Testament (although very rarely in the Old Testament). But,
more basically, belief in the resurrection arises as a corollary of faith in
the sovereign purpose of God, which is not restricted by death and which
holds man in being beyond his natural mortality. In the words of Martin
Luther, "Anyone with whom God speaks, whether in wrath or in mercy,
the same is certainly immortal. The Person of God who speaks, and the
Word, show that we are creatures with whom God wills to speak, right
into eternity, and in an immortal manner."[12] In a similar vein it is argued
that if it be God's plan to create finite persons to exist in fellowship with
himself, then it contradicts both his own intention and his love for the
creatures made in his image if he allows men to pass out of existence
when his purpose for them remains largely unfulfilled.

It is this promised fulfillment of God's purpose for man, in which the
full possibilities of human nature will be realized, that constitutes the

---

[10] For example, Irenaeus, *Against Heresies,* Book II, Chap. 34, para. 1.

[11] I Corinthians, 15:37.

[12] Quoted by Emil Brunner, *Dogmatics,* II, 69.

"heaven" symbolized in the New Testament as a joyous banquet in which all and sundry rejoice together. As we saw when discussing the problem of evil, no theodicy can succeed without drawing into itself this eschatological [13] faith in an eternal, and therefore infinite, good which thus outweighs all the pains and sorrows that have been endured on the way to it.

Balancing the idea of heaven in Christian tradition is the idea of hell. This, too, is relevant to the problem of theodicy. For just as the reconciling of God's goodness and power with the fact of evil requires that out of the travail of history there shall come in the end an eternal good for man, so likewise it would seem to preclude man's eternal misery. The only kind of evil that is finally incompatible with God's unlimited power and love would be utterly pointless and wasted suffering, pain which is never redeemed and worked into the fulfilling of God's good purpose. Unending torment would constitute precisely such suffering; for being eternal, it could never lead to a good end beyond itself. Thus, hell as conceived by its enthusiasts, such as Augustine or Calvin, is a major part of the problem of evil! If hell is construed as eternal torment, the theological motive behind the idea is directly at variance with the urge to seek a theodicy. However, it is by no means clear that the doctrine of eternal punishment can claim a secure New Testament basis.[14] If, on the other hand, "hell" means a continuation of the purgatorial suffering often experienced in this life, and leading eventually to the high good of heaven, it no longer stands in conflict with the needs of theodicy. Again, the idea of hell may be deliteralized and valued as a *mythos,* as a powerful and pregnant symbol of the grave responsibility inherent in man's freedom in relation to his Maker.

DOES PARAPSYCHOLOGY HELP?

The spiritualist movement claims that life after death has been proved by well-attested cases of communication between the living and the "dead."

During the closing quarter of the nineteenth century and the decades of the present century this claim has been made the subject of careful and prolonged study by a number of responsible and competent persons.[15] This work, which may be approximately dated from the founding

13 From the Greek *eschaton,* end.

14 The Greek word *aionios,* which is used in the New Testament and which is usually translated as "eternal" or "everlasting," can bear either this meaning or the more limited meaning of "for the aeon, or age."

15 The list of past presidents of the Society for Psychical Research includes the philosophers Henri Bergson, William James, Hans Driesch, Henry Sidgwick, F. C. S. Schiller, C. D. Broad, and H. H. Price; the psychologists William McDougall, Gardner Murphy, Franklin Prince, and R. H. Thouless; the physicists Sir William Crookes, Sir Oliver Lodge, Sir William Barrett, and Lord Rayleigh; and the classicist Gilbert Murray.

in London of the Society for Psychical Research in 1882, is known either by the name adopted by that society or in the United States by the name parapsychology.

Approaching the subject from the standpoint of our interest in this chapter, we may initially divide the phenomena studied by the parapsychologist into two groups. There are those phenomena that involve no reference to the idea of a life after death, chief among these being psychokinesis and extrasensory perception (ESP) in its various forms (such as telepathy, clairvoyance, and precognition). And there are those phenomena that raise the question of personal survival after death, such as the apparitions and other sensory manifestations of dead persons and the "spirit messages" received through mediums. This division is, however, only of preliminary use, for ESP has emerged as a clue to the understanding of much that occurs in the second group. We shall begin with a brief outline of the reasons that have induced the majority of workers in this field to be willing to postulate so strange an occurrence as telepathy.

Telepathy is a name for the mysterious fact that sometimes a thought in the mind of one person apparently causes a similar thought to occur to someone else when there are no normal means of communication between them, and under circumstances such that mere coincidence seems to be excluded.

For example, one person may draw a series of pictures or diagrams on paper and somehow transmit an impression of these to someone else in another room who then draws recognizable reproductions of them. This might well be a coincidence in the case of a single successful reproduction; but can a series consist entirely of coincidences?

Experiments have been devised to measure the probability of chance coincidence in supposed cases of telepathy. In the simplest of these, cards printed in turn with five different symbols are used. A pack of fifty, consisting of ten bearing each symbol, is then thoroughly shuffled, and the sender concentrates on the cards one at a time while the receiver (who of course can see neither sender nor cards) tries to write down the correct order of symbols. This procedure is repeated, with constant reshuffling, hundreds or thousands of times. Since there are only five different symbols, a random guess would stand one chance in five of being correct. Consequently, on the assumption that only "chance" is operating, the receiver should be right in about 20 per cent of his tries, and wrong in about 80 per cent; and the longer the series, the closer should be the approach to this proportion. However, good telepathic subjects are right in a far larger number of cases than can be reconciled with random guessing. The deviation from chance expectation can be converted mathematically into "odds against chance" (increasing as the proportion of hits is maintained over a longer and longer series of tries). In this way, odds of over a million to one have been recorded. J. B. Rhine (Duke University) has reported results showing "antichance" values ranging from seven (which equals odds against chance of 100,000 to one) to eighty-two (which converts the odds against chance to billions).[16] S. G. Soal (London University) has reported positive results for precognitive telepathy with odds against chance of $10^{35} \times 5$, or of billions to one.[17] Other researchers have also recorded confirming results.[18] In the light of these reports, it is difficult to deny that some positive factor, and not merely "chance," is operating. "Telepathy" is simply a name for this unknown positive factor.

How does telepathy operate? Only negative conclusions seem to be justified to date. It can, for example, be said with reasonable certainty that telepathy does not consist in any kind of physical radiation, analogous to radio waves. For, first, telepathy is not delayed or weakened in proportion to distance, as are all known forms of radiation; and, second, there is no organ in the brain or elsewhere that can plausibly be regarded as its sending or receiving center. Telepathy appears to be a purely mental occurrence.

It is not, however, a matter of transferring or transporting a thought out of one mind into another—if, indeed, such an idea makes sense at all. The telepathized thought does not leave the sender's consciousness in order to enter that of the receiver. What happens would be better described by saying that the sender's thought gives rise to a mental "echo" in the mind of the receiver. This "echo" occurs at the unconscious level, and consequently the version of it that rises into the receiver's consciousness may be only fragmentary and may be distorted or symbolized in various ways, as in dreams.

According to one theory that has been tentatively suggested to explain telepathy, our minds are separate and mutually insulated only at the conscious (and preconscious) level. But at the deepest level of the unconscious, we are constantly influencing one another, and it is at this level that telepathy takes place.[19]

---

[16] J. B. Rhine, *Extrasensory Perception* (Boston: Society for Psychical Research, 1935), Table XLIII, p. 162. See also Rhine, *New Frontiers of the Mind* (New York: Farrar and Rinehart, Inc., 1937), pp. 69f.

[17] S. G. Soal, *Proceedings of the Society for Psychical Research,* XLVI, 152–98 and XLVII, 21–150. See also S. G. Soal's *The Experimental Situation in Psychical Research* (London: The Society for Psychical Research, 1947).

[18] For surveys of the experimental work, see Whately Carrington, *Telepathy* (London: Methuen & Co. Ltd., 1945); G. N. M. Tyrrell, *The Personality of Man* (London: Penguin Books Ltd., 1946); S. G. Soal and F. Bateman, *Modern Experiments in Telepathy* (London: Faber & Faber Ltd. and New Haven, Conn.: Yale University Press, 1954); and for important Russian work, L. L. Vasiliev, *Experiments in Mental Suggestion,* 1962 (Church Crookham: Institute for the Study of Mental Images, 1963—English translation).

[19] Whately Carrington, *Telepathy* (London: Methuen & Co. Ltd., 1945), Chaps. 6–8.

How is a telepathized thought directed to one particular receiver among so many? Apparently the thoughts are directed by some link of emotion or common interest. For example, two friends are sometimes telepathically aware of any grave crisis or shock experienced by the other, even though they are at opposite ends of the earth.

We shall turn now to the other branch of parapsychology, which has more obvious bearing upon our subject. The *Proceedings of the Society for Psychical Research* contain a large number of carefully recorded and satisfactorily attested cases of the appearance of the figure of someone who has recently died to living people (in rare instances to more than one at a time) who were, in many cases, at a distance and unaware of the death. The S.P.R. reports also establish beyond reasonable doubt that the minds that operate in the mediumistic trance, purporting to be spirits of the departed, sometimes give personal information the medium could not have acquired by normal means and at times even give information, later verified, which had not been known to any living person.

On the other hand, physical happenings, such as the "materializations" of spirit forms in a visible and tangible form, are much more doubtful. But even if we discount the entire range of physical phenomena, it remains true that the best cases of trance utterance are impressive and puzzling, and taken at face value are indicative of survival and communication after death. If, through a medium, one talks with an intelligence that gives a coherent impression of being an intimately known friend who has died and who establishes identity by a wealth of private information and indefinable personal characteristics—as has occasionally happened—then we cannot dismiss without careful trial the theory that what is taking place is the return of a consciousness from the spirit world.

However, the advance of knowledge in the other branch of parapsychology, centering upon the study of extrasensory perception, has thrown unexpected light upon this apparent commerce with the departed. For it suggests that unconscious telepathic contact between the medium and his or her client is an important and possibly a sufficient explanatory factor. This was vividly illustrated by the experience of two women who decided to test the spirits by taking into their minds, over a period of weeks, the personality and atmosphere of an entirely imaginary character in an unpublished novel written by one of the women. After thus filling their minds with the characteristics of this fictitious person, they went to a reputable medium, who proceeded to describe accurately their imaginary friend as a visitant from beyond the grave and to deliver appropriate messages from him.

An even more striking case is that of the "direct voice" medium (i.e., a medium in whose séances the voice of the communicating "spirit" is heard apparently speaking out of the air) who produced the spirit of one "Gordon Davis" who spoke in his own recognizable voice, displayed considerable knowledge about Gordon Davis, and remembered his death. This was extremely impressive until it was discovered that Gordon Davis was still alive; he was, of all ghostly occupations, a real-estate agent, and had been trying to sell a house at the time when the séance took place![20]

Such cases suggest that genuine mediums are simply persons of exceptional telepathic sensitiveness who unconsciously derive the "spirits" from their clients' minds.

In connection with "ghosts," in the sense of apparitions of the dead, it has been established that there can be "meaningful hallucinations," the source of which is almost certainly telepathic. To quote a classic and somewhat dramatic example: a woman sitting by a lake sees the figure of a man running toward the lake and throwing himself in. A few days later a man commits suicide by throwing himself into this same lake. Presumably, the explanation of the vision is that the man's thought while he was contemplating suicide had been telepathically projected onto the scene via the woman's mind.[21]

In many of the cases recorded there is delayed action. The telepathically projected thought lingers in the recipient's unconscious mind until a suitable state of inattention to the outside world enables it to appear to his conscious mind in a dramatized form—for example, by a hallucinatory voice or vision—by means of the same mechanism that operates in dreams.

If phantoms of the living can be created by previously experienced thoughts and emotions of the person whom they represent, the parallel possibility arises that phantoms of the dead are caused by thoughts and emotions that were experienced by the person represented when he was alive. In other words, ghosts may be "psychic footprints," a kind of mental trace left behind by the dead, but not involving the presence or even the continued existence of those whom they represent.

These considerations tend away from the hopeful view that parapsychology will open a window onto another world. However, it is too early for a final verdict; and in the meantime one should be careful not to confuse absence of knowledge with knowledge of absence.[22]

---

[20] S. G. Soal, "A Report of Some Communications Received through Mrs. Blanche Cooper," Sec. 4, *Proceedings of the Society for Psychical Research,* XXXV, 560–89.

[21] F. W. H. Myers, *Human Personality and Its Survival of Bodily Death* (London: Longmans, Green, & Co., 1903), I, 270–71.

[22] Perhaps the most thorough philosophical discussion of the subject is C. D. Broad's *Lectures on Psychical Research* (London: Routledge & Kegan Paul Ltd., and New York: Humanities Press, Inc., 1962).

CHAPTER EIGHT

Human Destiny: Karma and Reincarnation

THE POPULAR CONCEPT To nearly everyone formed by our Western Atlantic culture it seems self-evident that we came into existence at conception or birth and shall see the last of this world at death: in other words, we are born only once and we die only once. However, to one brought up within the Hindu culture of India it seems self-evident that we have, on the contrary, lived many times before and must live many times again in this world. Each idea or theory involves its own difficulties, and I shall be pointing out presently some of the difficulties in the idea of reincarnation. But first let us take note of the main difficulty that Indians see in the Western assumption. They point to the immense inequalities of human birth. One person is born with a healthy body and a high IQ, to loving parents with a good income in an advanced and affluent society, so that all the riches of human culture are open to him and he has considerable freedom to chose his own mode of life. Another is born with a crippled body and a low IQ, to unloving, unaffluent and uncultured parents in a society in which he is highly likely to become a criminal and to die an early and violent death. Is it fair that they should be born with such unequal advantages? If a new soul is created whenever a new baby is conceived, can the Creator who is responsible for each soul's unequal endowment be described as a loving creator? We have all heard the story of John Bradford, who saw a criminal being taken to be hung and said, "But for the grace of God there goes John Bradford." The story is edifying in so far as it reminds us of God's grace to John Bradford; but what about God's grace, or lack of grace, to the condemned criminal? The more one contemplates the gross inequalities of human birth, and our Western religious assumption that human beings are divinely created in these different conditions, the more one is likely to see a grave problem here.

The alternative assumption of the Indian religions is that we have all lived before and that the conditions of our present life are a direct consequence of our previous lives. There is no arbitrariness, no randomness, no injustice in the inequalities of our human lot, but only cause and effect, the reaping now of what we have ourselves sown in the past. Our essential self continues from life to life, being repeatedly reborn or reincarnated, the state of its karma determining the circumstances of its next life.

In its more popular form in both East and West the doctrine of rein-- carnation holds that the conscious character-bearing and (in principle) memory-bearing self transmigrates from body to body. As we read in the *Bhagavad Gita,* "Just as a person casts off worn-out garments and puts on others that are new, even so does the embodied soul cast off worn-out bodies and takes on others that are new" (2, 13). On this conception it is possible to say that I—the "I" who am now conscious and who am now writing these words—have lived before and will live again, in other bodies. It must accordingly be in principle possible for me, in my present body, to remember my past lives, even though in fact the traumas of death and birth generally erase these memories, repressing them to a deep and normally inaccessible level of the unconscious. Occasionally, however, ordinary people do for some reason remember fragments of a recent life; and these claimed memories of former lives are important, not only as evidence offered for rebirth, but also conceptually, as fixing what is meant by the doctrine. One may or may not find cases of this kind to be impressive considered as hard evidence for rebirth. Nevertheless, the fact that supposed recollections of former lives are pointed to as evidence does mark out a particular content for the idea of rebirth.[1] Let me, therefore, formulate a reincarnation hypothesis on the basis of these instances of claimed memories of former lives.

Consider the relation between the John Hick who is now writing, whom I shall call J. H.[50], and John Hick at the age of two, whom I shall call J. H.[2]. The main differences between them are, first, that J. H.[50] and

---

[1] There is an extensive literature reporting and discussing such cases. One of the few books of real value to a critically trained reader is Ian Stevenson, *Twenty Cases Suggestive of Reincarnation* (New York: American Society for Psychical Research, 1966).

J. H.[2] do not look at all like each other and, second, that their conscious selves are quite different. As to the first difference, no one shown a photo of J. H.[2] would know, without being told, that it is a photo of J. H.[50] as he was forty-eight years ago, rather than that of almost anybody else at the age of two. For there is very little similarity of appearance between these two visible objects. And as to the second difference, if one were to hear a recording of the two-year old J. H. revealing his thoughts in words and other noises, one would, I think, feel that the present J. H.[50] has a very different mind. No doubt the same basic personality traits are present in both the child and the man, but nevertheless the conscious self of the one is very different from the conscious self of the other—so much so that a comparison of the two would never by itself lead us to conclude that they are the same self. There are, then, immense differences between J. H.[2] and J. H.[50] from the points of view both of physical and of psychological description. But notwithstanding that, J. H.[50] does have at least one fragmentary memory of an event that was experienced by J. H.[2]. He remembers being told when his sister, who is two years younger than himself, was born. Thus there is a tenuous memory link connecting J. H.[50] with J. H.[2] despite all the dissimilarities that we have noted between them; and this fact reminds us that it is possible to speak of memory across the gap of almost any degree of physical and psychological difference.

Now let us see if we can say the same of someone who remembers a previous life. To spell this out in the well-known case of Shanti Devi: Lugdi—who was born in 1902, lived in Muthra, and married Kedar Nath Chaubey—was (presumably) very different as regards both physical and psychological descriptions from Shanti Devi who was born in 1926 and lived at Delhi. But Shanti Devi had (or claimed to have) certain memories of people and events experienced by Lugdi, which are said to have been confirmed by impartial investigators. And our reincarnation hypothesis is that despite the differences between them, they are in fact the same person or self, in a sense comparable with that in which J. H.[50] is the same person as J. H.[2]. In speaking in this way of the same person being born in 1902 in one part of India, later dying, and then being born again in 1926 in another part of India, we are presupposing the existence of a continuing mental entity which I am calling the self or the person. The hypothesis we are considering is that just as J. H.[50] is the same person as J. H.[2], though at a later point in the history of that person, so also is Shanti Devi the same person as Lugdi, though at a later point in that person's history. The big difference—concerning which we have to ask whether it is *too* big a difference—is that now these are not earlier and later points in the same life but in two successive lives. They are, as it were, points in different volumes of the same multivolume work instead of in different chapters of the same volume.

Let us, then, consider the claim that all human selves have lived many times before, even though the great majority, even perhaps some 99 percent, have no memory of any such previous lives. And the question that I want to raise concerns the criterion or criteria by which someone living today is said to be the same person or self as someone who lived, let us say, 500 years ago of whom he has no knowledge or memory. For when we remove the connecting thread of memory, as we are doing in our present rebirth hypothesis, we have taken away one, and a very important one, of the three strands of continuity that constitute what we normally mean by the identity of a human individual through time. A second strand is bodily continuity, an unbroken existence through space and time from the newly born baby to the old man, a continuity stretching thus from the cradle to the grave. It may be that none of the atoms that composed the baby's body are now part of the adult's body. But nonetheless a continuously changing physical organism has existed and has been in principle observable, composed from moment to moment of slightly different populations of atoms, but with sufficient overlap of population and of configuration of population from moment to moment for it to constitute the same organism. However, this strand of bodily continuity is also taken away by our rebirth hypothesis, for there is no physical connection between someone living in the United States today and someone who lived, say, in ancient Greece two and a half thousand years ago. Nor does it even seem to be claimed by the doctrine of rebirth that there is any bodily resemblance; for it is said that one is sometimes born as a man, sometimes as a woman, sometimes in one and sometimes in another branch of the human race, and sometimes indeed (according to one version of the doctrine) as an animal or perhaps as an insect.

Thus, all that is left to be the bearer of personal identity is the third strand, which is the psychological continuity of a pattern of mental dispositions. It is this that now has to carry all the weight of the identity of two persons, one of whom is said to be a reincarnation of the other. For the only connection left, when memory and bodily continuity are excluded, lies in the psychological dispositions that constitute one's personal character. It is claimed that B, who is A reincarnated, has the same personality traits as A. If A was proud and intolerant, B will be proud and intolerant. If A becomes in the course of his life a great artist, B will start life with a strong artistic propensity. If A was kind and thoughtful, B will be kind and thoughtful. But much now depends, for the viability of the theory, upon the *degree* of similarity that is claimed to exist between the total personality of A at t^1 and the total personality of B at t^2. Many people are kind and thoughtful, or have artistic temperaments, or are proud and intolerant; but as long as they are distinct bodily beings with distinct and different streams of consciousness and memory, the fact that two individuals exhibit a common character trait, or even a number of such traits, does not lead us to identify them as the same person. In the case of people living at the same time, to do so would be a direct violation of the concept of "same person." In the case of people who are not alive at the same time such an identification is not ruled out with the same a priori logical definitiveness; but in spite of that, it is beset with the most formidable difficulties. For the similarity between A (t^1) and B (t^2) must, in most cases, be so general as to be capable of numerous different exemplifications, since A and B may be of different races and sexes, and products of different civilizations, climates, and historical epochs. There can be *general* similarities of character, found in such qualities as selfishness and unselfishness, introverted or extroverted types of personality, artistic or practical bents, and in level of intelligence, between, let us say, a female Tibetan peasant of the twelfth century B.C. and a male American college graduate of the twentieth century A.D. But such general similarities would never by themselves lead or entitle us to identify the two as the same person. Indeed, to make an identity claim on these grounds—in a case in which there is neither bodily continuity nor any link of memory—would commit us to the principle that all individuals who are not alive at the same time and who exhibit rather similar personality patterns are to be regarded as the same person. But in that case there would be far too many people who qualify under this criterion as being the same person. How many people of Lugdi's generation were as much like Shanti Devi in general character as Lugdi was? Probably many hundreds of thousands. How many people in the last generation before I was born had character traits similar to those that I have? Probably many hundreds of thousands. On this basis alone, then, it would never have occurred to anyone that Lugdi and Shanti Devi were the same person, or that I am the same person as any one particular individual in the past. On this basis I could equally as well be a reincarnation of any one of many thousands of people in each past generation. Thus, this criterion of character similarity is far too broad and permissive; if it establishes anything, it establishes much too much and becomes self-defeating.

Thus the idea of reincarnation, in the sense of the transmigration of the self (though normally without memory of its previous lives) from death in one body to birth in another, is beset by conceptual difficulties of the gravest kind.

THE VEDĀNTIC CONCEPTION
Let us then now turn to the more complex and subtle conception of reincarnation taught in Hindu Vedāntic philosophy. This is, of course, by no means the only school of Indian religious thought; but the Vedāntic conception of karma and rebirth is a central one from which most of the other schools differ only

marginally. According to Advaita Vedānta, the ultimate reality—Brahman —is pure undifferentiated consciousness, beyond all qualities including personality. The creative power of Brahman, called *māyā,* expresses itself in the existence of the universe, whose nature is *māyā,* which now connotes unreality in the sense of being dependent and temporary. The infinite eternal consciousness becomes associated with *māyā* to constitute a plurality of temporary finite consciousnesses, *jīvātmans* or *jīvas,* which I shall call souls. These finite consciousnesses are products of *māyā,* and their very existence is a kind of illusion, the illusion namely of separateness from the one universal consciousness. In an often used Vedāntic simile, *Brahman* is like Space and the individual souls are like space in jars. When the jars are destroyed, the space that they enclosed remains part of Space. Likewise, the souls merge into the infinite *Brahman* when the ignorance that constitutes their finite boundaries is removed in enlightenment.

There are, then, a limitless number of individual souls; and yet this plurality and individuality is ultimately illusory, for when different souls attain to consciousness of themselves as *Brahman,* the distinction between them ceases to exist: all souls as *Brahman* are one and the same. And the theory of karma and rebirth is concerned with the soul and its evolution from the state of illusion to true self-consciousness. For the innumerable souls, as "sparks of divinity" that have become illusorily separated from their source, ground, and identity in *Brahman,* are being gradually purged of this illusion through a succession of rebirths, in a process that is eventually to culminate in the attainment of liberation and the realization of identity with the sole ultimate Reality, *Brahman,* unspoiled by any illusory sense of separate identity. (This conception has, of course, its affinities in the West in Neoplatonism and Gnosticism and in the recent theology of Paul Tillich).

There are, then, an infinity of souls existing beginninglessly throughout past time. But I, the conscious self now writing, and you, the conscious self now reading, are not—or rather are not consciously—any of these eternal souls. We are psychophysical egos, illusorily distinct persons of the kind that exist only in this realm of *māyā.* For whereas the psychophysical ego is a man or a woman, the soul is neither male or female, but includes (in Jung's terminology) the *animus* and *anima* aspects that, when embodied in varying proportions, constitute human masculinity and femininity. Again, whereas the psychophysical ego is not normally conscious of the eternal past of the soul, there are depths of the soul in which all this past experience is recorded. Each psychophysical ego is thus a temporary expression, or organ, or instrument of an eternal soul, one indeed of the succession of such expressions which constitute the successive rebirths of that soul. For that the soul is involved in *māyā* means that it has become enclosed in a set of "bodies" or coverings, thought of on the analogy of a number of sheaths successively enclosing the blade of a sword, and all having to be discarded before the blade is free. There are three principal such "bodies" or sheaths: the gross body (*sthūla śarīra*), the subtle body (*sūksma śarīra* or *liṅga śarīra*) and the causal body (*kārana śarīra*). So far as the essential logic of the idea of rebirth is concerned we can conflate the latter two into one, the "subtle body," and concentrate upon the relation between this and the "gross body." The "gross body" is the physical organism that begins to be formed at conception and begins to disintegrate at death. But it is survived by the "subtle body," which then influences the development of another physical body as its next vehicle or incarnation. It must, however, at once be added that the phrase "subtle body" is liable to be seriously misleading to the western mind. For the "subtle body" is not, in the philosophically sophisticated versions of the theory, conceived of as a material entity in the western sense of "material." It does not occupy space, has no shape or size, and is indeed not a body at all in our Western sense of the term. It is, however, material in the quite different sense given by the fundamental Indian dichotomy between consciousness and everything that lacks consciousness and is called *prakṛti* —"nature" or "matter"—this being identical with *māyā*. In western terms the subtle body must accordingly be described as a mental rather than as a physical entity; and indeed one Hindu expositor speaks of it simply as "the psychical part of the psychophysical organism."[2] So far as its functions in the theory of rebirth are concerned, we may describe the *liṅga śarīra* as a mental entity of substance that is modified by, or registers and thus (metaphorically) "embodies," the moral, aesthetic, intellectual, and spiritual dispositions that have been built up in the course of living a human life, or rather in living a succession of human, and perhaps also nonhuman, lives. These modifications of the subtle body are called *saṃskāras*, impressions. But they are not thought of on the analogy of static impressions, like marks on paper, but rather as dynamic impressions, modifications of a living organism expressed in its pattern of behavior. We ordinarily think of the human mind and personality as being modified in all sorts of ways by its own volitions and its responses to its experience. A repeated indulgence in selfish policies reinforces one's egoistic tendencies; a constant exercise of the discipline of precise thought makes for more lucid and exact thinking; devoted attention to one or another of the arts quickens and deepens one's aesthetic sensibilities; spiritual meditation opens the self to the influence of a larger environment; and so on. These familiar facts can be expressed by saying that the *liṅga śarīra* is the seat of the various

[2] Suryanarayana Sastri, "The Doctrine of Reincarnation in Educational Work," *Indian Philosophical Annual,* 1965, p. 165. This volume of the *Annual* contains the Proceedings of an All-India Seminar held at the University of Madras in 1965, devoted to the subject of "Karma and Rebirth."

emotional, spiritual, moral, aesthetic, and intellectual modifications that are happening to us all the time in the course of our human existence. Such modifications are most adequately characterized in contemporary Western categories as mental dispositions.

We have already noted that the subtle body belongs to the material (*prakṛti*) side of the fundamental dichotomy between consciousness and *prakṛti;* and it is for this reason that it is appropriate in the context of Indian thought to call it a body. For being finite, changeable, and devoid of consciousness, it has far more in common with the physical body than with the soul. To appreciate this we have to conceive of thoughts, emotions, and desires as things, and as things capable of existing apart from consciousness as dispositional energies that, when linked with consciousness, can guide action. Through like grouping with like in mutual reinforcement, such dispositions form relatively stable and enduring structures whose "shape" is the character of the person whose thoughts have formed it. Such a dispositional structure survives the extinction of consciousness in death and continues to exist as an entity, the subtle body or *liṅga śarīra,* which will later become linked to a new conscious organism. It is thus very close to what C. D. Broad has called the "psychic factor."[3] Broad developed his concept of the psychic factor to provide a possible explanation of the phenomenon of trance mediumship. When an individual dies, the mental aspect of his being persists, not however as a complete conscious personality, but as a constellation of mental elements—dispositions, memories, desires, fears, etc.,—constituting a psychic factor, which may hold together for a considerable time or may quickly disintegrate into scattered fragments. Broad suggested that such a psychic grouping, sufficiently cohesive to be identified as consisting of the memories and dispositional character of a particular deceased individual, may become connected with a medium in a state of trance, thus generating a temporary conscious personality that is a conflation of certain persisting mental elements of the deceased together with the living structure of the medium. The theory of reincarnation can be seen as taking this concept further—as indeed Broad himself noted[4]—and claiming that the psychic factor that separates itself from the body at death subsequently becomes fused, not with the developed life structure of a medium, but with the still undeveloped life structure of a human embryo. It then influences the growth of the embryo, as a factor additional to its physical genetic inheritance.

If we ask why Hindus believe that this is a true account of the facts of human existence, there are three interlocking answers. One is that it is a revealed truth taught in the Vedas. A second is that reincarnation is an

---

[3] C. D. Broad, *The Mind and Its Place in Nature* (London: Routledge & Kegan Paul Ltd., 1925), pp. 536ff.

[4] Ibid., p. 551.

hypothesis that makes sense of many aspects of human life, including the inequalities of human birth; I shall return to this presently. And the third is that there are the fragmentary memories of former lives to which I have already referred and also, even more importantly, the much fuller memories that are attained by those who have achieved *mokṣa,* liberation and enlightenment. It is claimed that the yoga, when he attains, remembers all his former lives and sees for himself the karmic connection that runs through a succession of apparently different and unrelated lives. This last item is for many in India the most important of all grounds for belief in reincarnation.

But now, I want to ask, what exactly does reincarnation mean when it is thus given factual anchorage by a claimed retrospective yogic memory of a series of lives that were not linked by memory while they were being lived? The picture before us is of, say, a thousand distinct empirical selves living their different lives one after another and being as distinct from each other as any other set of a thousand lives; and yet differing from a random series of a thousand lives in that the last member of the series attains a level of consciousness at which he is aware of the entire series. Further, he remembers the entire series as lives which he, now in this higher state of awareness, has himself lived. And yet there is something logically odd about such "remembering," which prompts one to put it in quotation marks. For this higher state of consciousness did not experience those earlier lives and therefore it cannot in any ordinary sense be said to remember them. It is in a state as though it had experienced them, although in fact it did not.

The claim here, then, is that there will in the future exist a supernormal state of consciousness, in which "memories" of a long succession of different lives occur. But this leaves open the question of how best to describe such a state of affairs. Let us name the first person in the series A, and the last Z. Are we to say that B–Z are a series of reincarnations of A? If we do, we shall be implicitly stipulating the following definition: given two or more noncontemporaneous human lives, if there is a higher consciousness in which they are all "remembered," then each later individual in the series is defined as being a reincarnation of each earlier individual. But reincarnation so defined is a concept far removed from the idea that if I am A, then *I* shall be repeatedly reborn as B–Z. For there is no conceptual reason why we should stipulate that the different lives must be noncontemporaneous. If it is possible for a higher consciousness to "remember" any number of different lives, there seems in principle to be no reason why it should not "remember" lives that have been going on at the same time as easily as lives that have been going on at different times. Indeed, we can conceive of an unlimited higher consciousness in which "memories" occur of all human lives that have ever been lived. Then *all* human lives, however different from their own several points of view, would be connected via a higher consciousness in the way postulated by the idea of reincarnation. It would then be proper to say of *any* two lives, whether earlier and later, later and earlier, or contemporaneous, that the one individual is a different incarnation of the other. Thus it seems that there are considerable conceptual difficulties in the idea of reincarnation in its more subtle Vedāntic form as well as in its more popular form.

Let us now return to the inequalities of human birth and ask whether the idea of reincarnation can after all really help to explain these. Either there is a first life, characterized by initial human differences; or else (as in the Vedāntic philosophy) there is no first life, but a beginningless regress of incarnations, in which case the explanation of the inequalities of our present life is endlessly postponed and never achieved. For we are no nearer to an ultimate explanation of the circumstances of our present birth when we are told that they are consequences of a previous life if that previous life has in turn to be explained by reference to a yet previous life, and that by reference to another, and so on, in an infinite regress. One can affirm the beginningless character of the soul's existence in this way; but one cannot then claim that it renders either intelligible or morally acceptable the inequalities found in our present human lot. For the solution has not been produced but only postponed to infinity. And if instead we were to postulate a first life (as Hinduism does not), we should then have to hold either that souls are created as identical psychic atoms or else as embodying, at least in germ, the differences that have subsequently developed. If the latter, the problem of human inequality arises in full force at the point of that initial creation; if the former, it arises as forcefully with regard to the environment that has produced all the manifold differences that have subsequently arisen between initially identical units. Thus if there is a divine Creator, it would seem that he cannot escape along any of these paths from an ultimate responsibility for the character of his creation, including the gross inequalities inherent within it.

A DEMYTHOLOGIZED The possibility of construing reincarnation as an un-
INTERPRETATION verifiable and unfalsifiable metaphysical idea takes
us to the borders of a third form of the doctrine. In this form it is a mythological expression of the fact that all our actions have effects upon some part of the human community, and have to be borne, for good or ill, by others in the future. It is this ethical sense that has been attributed to the Buddha by some scholars, and notably by J. C. Jennings, formerly vice-chancellor of Patna University.[5] Jennings says, "Disbelieving in the permanence of the individual soul he [the Buddha] could not accept the

[5] J. C. Jennings, *The Vedāntic Buddhism of the Buddha* (London: Oxford University Press, 1948).

Hindu doctrine of Karma implying the transmigration of the soul at death to a new body; but believing fully in moral responsibility and the consequences of all acts, words, and thoughts, he fully accepted the doctrine of Karma in another sense, implying the transmission of the effects of actions from one generation of men to all succeeding generations" (p. xlvii). Again, Jennings says, "Assuming the common origin and the fundamental unity of all life and spirit, he [the Buddha] assumed the unity of the force of Karma upon the living material of the whole world, and the doctrine of Karma taught by him is collective and not individual" (p. xxv).

On this view karma, with reincarnation as its mythological expression, is really a moral truth, a teaching of universal human responsibility. All our deeds affect the human future, as the life of each of us has in its turn been affected by those who have lived before us. Instead of individual threads of karmic history there is a common karma of humanity, to which each contributes and by which each is affected. Understood in this manner, the idea of reincarnation is a way of affirming the corporate unity of the human race, and the responsibility of each toward the whole of which he is a part. We are not monadic individuals, each one a separate island to himself, but mutually interacting parts of the one human world in which the thoughts and acts of each reverberate continually for good or ill through the lives of others. As the ways in which men have lived in the past have formed the world in which we now have to live, so we in turn are now forming the world in which future generations will have to dwell. And as our inherited world, or state of world karma, has formed us as individuals born into it, so we in turn are helping to shape the environment that is to form those who live after us. So conceived, the idea of karma has immense practical implications at a time when the nations are grappling with the threat of the pollution of our human environment, with problems of environmental planning and conservation, with the prevention of nuclear war, with the control of the population explosion, with racial conflict, and with so many other problems concerned about the ways in which the actions of each individual and group affect the welfare of all. Seen in this way, karma is an ethical doctrine. And both the more popular idea of the transmigration of souls and the more philosophical idea of the continuity of a "subtle body" from individual to individual in succeeding generations can be seen as mythological expressions of this great moral truth.

Most western philosophers would probably have no difficulty in accepting this last form of reincarnation doctrine. For it is a vivid affirmation of human unity; and the world today is such that if we do not unite in a common life, we are only too likely to find ourselves united in a common death. But to what extent this is an acceptable interpretation of the idea of rebirth, which has for some thousands of years been cherished by the great religions of India, is not for us to say.

CHAPTER NINE

The Conflicting Truth Claims of Different Religions

MANY FAITHS, ALL CLAIMING TO BE TRUE

Until comparatively recently each of the different religions of the world had developed in substantial ignorance of the others. There have been, it is true, great movements of expansion which have brought two faiths into contact: above all, the expansion of Buddhism during the last three centuries B.C. and the early centuries of the Christian era, carrying its message throughout India and Southeast Asia and into China, Tibet, and Japan, and then, the resurgence of Hindu religion at the expense of Buddhism, with the result that today Buddhism is rarely to be found on the Indian subcontinent; next, the first Christian expansion into the Roman Empire; then the expansion of Islam in the seventh and eighth centuries C.E. into the Middle East, Europe, and later India; and finally, the second expansion of Christianity in the missionary movement of the nineteenth century. But these interactions were for the most part conflicts rather than dialogues; they did not engender any deep or sympathetic understanding of one faith by the theologians of another. It is only during the last hundred years or so that the scholarly study of world religions has made possible an accurate appreciation of the faiths of other men, and so has brought home to an increasing number of people the problem of the conflicting truth claims made by different religious traditions. This issue now emerges as a major topic demanding a prominent place on the agenda of the philosopher of religion today and in the future.

The problem can be posed very concretely in this way. If I had been born in India, I would probably be a Hindu; if in Egypt, probably a Muslim; if in Ceylon, probably a Buddhist; but I was born in England and am, predictably, a Christian. But these different religions seem to say different and incompatible things about the nature of ultimate reality, about the modes of divine activity, and about the nature and destiny of man. Is the divine nature personal or nonpersonal? Does deity become incarnate in the world? Are human beings reborn again and again on earth? Is the empirical self the real self, destined for eternal life in fellowship with God, or is it only a temporary and illusory manifestation of an eternal higher self? Is the Bible, or the Koran, or the Bhagavad Gita the Word of God? If what Christianity says in answer to such questions is true, must not what Hinduism says be to a large extent false? If what Buddhism says is true, must not what Islam says be largely false?

The sceptical thrust of these questions goes very deep; for it is a short step from the thought that the different religions cannot all be true, although they each claim to be, to the thought that in all probability none of them is true. Thus Hume laid down the principle "that, in matters of religion, whatever is different is contrary; and that it is impossible the religions of ancient Rome, of Turkey, of Siam, and of China should, all of them, be established on any solid foundation." Accordingly, regarding miracles as evidence for the truth of a particular faith, "Every miracle, therefore, pretended to have been wrought in any of these religions (and all of them abound in miracles), as its direct scope is to establish the particular religion to which it is attributed; so has it the same force, though more indirectly, to overthrow every other system."[1] By the same reasoning, any grounds for believing a particular religion to be true must operate as grounds for believing every other religion to be false; and accordingly, for any particular religion, there will always be far more grounds for believing it to be false than for believing it to be true. This is the sceptical argument that arises from the conflicting truth claims of the various world faiths.

W. A. CHRISTIAN'S ANALYSIS   In his book *Meaning and Truth in Religion*[2], W. A. Christian begins with the idea of a "proposal for belief." Belief is here distinguished from knowledge; if I look at my watch and tell you the time, or if I look out of the window

---

1 David Hume, *An Enquiry Concerning Human Understanding*, para. 95
2 W. A. Christian, *Meaning and Truth in Religion* (Princeton, N.J.: Princeton University Press, 1964). See also Christian's *Oppositions of Religious Doctrines: A Study in the Logic of Dialogue Among Religions* (London: Macmillan & Co. Ltd. and New York: Herder and Herder, Inc., 1972).

and report that it is raining, I am giving information, not making a belief proposal in Christian's sense. The context in which proposals for belief are made is that of common interest in a question to which neither party knows the answer, and in relation to which there is accordingly scope for theories that would provide an answer. Such a theory, offered for positive acceptance, is a proposal for belief. The following are examples of well-known religious belief-proposals:

> *Jesus is the Messiah*
> *Atman is Brahman*
> *Allah is merciful*
> *All the Buddhas are one*

These examples are drawn respectively from Christianity, Hinduism, Islam, and Buddhism. It is clear that these belief-proposals are all different; but are they incompatible? Do they, as put forward by these different faiths, conflict with one another?

Consider first what looks like a very direct religious disagreement. Christians say that (A) "Jesus is the Messiah," whereas Jews say that Jesus is not the Messiah, and the Messiah is still to come. But William Christian points out that when we take account of what each party means by the term "Messiah" it turns out that they are not directly contradicting one another after all. For "Jews mean by 'the Messiah' a nondivine being who will restore Israel as an earthly community and usher in the consummation of history. Christians mean a promised savior of mankind from sin. Two different Messiah concepts are being expressed; hence two different propositions are being asserted."[3] And so when the Jew denies that Jesus is the Messiah, he is not denying what the Christian is asserting when he asserts that Jesus *is* the Messiah.

This could suggest the following view: the concepts used in the belief-proposals of a particular religion are peculiar to that religion. Christians use the concept of the Messiah (= divine savior); Jews, the concept of Messiah (= human agent of God's purposes); Buddhists, the concept of Nirvana; Hindus, the concept of Brahman; and Muslims, the concept of Falāh. But each of these ideas, as it occurs within these religions, gains its meaning from its use within the context of that religion and is thus peculiar to it and has meaning only as part of its discourse. Hence there cannot be a case of two religions employing the same concept and saying contradictory things about it. The Christian, for example, does not say that Allah is not merciful; for Allah is not a Christian concept and Christian discourse does not include any statements about Allah. Or again, the

[3] *Meaning and Truth in Religion,* pp. 15–16.

Muslim does not say that Atman is not Brahman; for the question does not arise within the circle of Islamic discourse.

This position could be developed along lines for which some have found inspiration in the later writings of Wittgenstein. Each religion, one might say, is a "form of life" with its own "language game." Christian language— employing such distinctively Christian concepts as Incarnation, Son of God, and Trinity—derives its meaning from the part that it plays in the Christian life. The criteria of what it is appropriate to say, and thus of what is to be accepted as true, are peculiar to this realm of discourse. These rules of the Christian language game, for example, treat the Bible and Christian tradition as important sources of knowledge. But nothing that is said in the context of Christian faith can either agree or disagree with anything that is said within the context of another religion. The Christian and, say, the Buddhist are different people, belonging to different religious communities and traditions, and speaking different religious languages, each of which has meaning in the context of a different religious form of life; accordingly there is no question of their making rival belief-proposals. Such a theory has the great attraction that it avoids entirely the otherwise vexing problems of the apparently conflicting truth claims made by different religions.

However, William Christian goes on to show that any such solution would be only apparent. Returning to our original example, it is true that Jews and Christians mean different things by "the Messiah" and thus that when the one says that Jesus is not the Messiah and the other that he *is,* they are not directly contradicting each other. But we can go behind these two Messiah concepts. We can speak of "the one whom God promised to send to redeem Israel," it being left open whether this is a human or a divine being. We then have the belief-proposal (B), "Jesus is the one whom God promised to send to redeem Israel," this being a proposal which the Christian accepts and the Jew rejects. At this point there is a real disagreement between them about the truth concerning Jesus, a disagreement that was only temporarily masked by noting the different concepts of Messiah that were in use. Indeed, if there were no such genuine and substantial disagreement, it would be difficult to account for the original splitting off of Christianity from Judaism and for the religious polemics that followed. The persisting disagreement does not have to involve any hostility or bitterness; it does not have to prevent Christians and Jews from rejoicing in all that they have in common; and it is compatible with close friendship and cooperation between them. But it is also clear that they do in fact hold different and incompatible beliefs about the nature and significance of Jesus—as also about a large number of other related matters.

Thus, whereas (A) "Jesus is the Messiah" has different meanings for Christian and Jew, when we go behind this formula to (B) "Jesus is the one whom God promised to send to redeem Israel," we find that at this point there is direct Jewish–Christian disagreement. And W. A. Christian points out that this process can be carried further to uncover differences between Christian and Jew on the one hand and, say, Stoics on the other. For it is a presupposition of (B) that (C) "The being who rules the world acts in history"; for he is said to "promise," to "send," and to "redeem Israel." But a Stoic would deny that the Divine does any of these things or indeed acts in history in any way. He thinks of the Divine in a quite different way so that the question, "Has God acted in history in such-and-such a manner?" can never arise: since the world–ruler does not act in history at all there is no scope for debate as to whether or not he has acted by sending Jesus.

This process of formulating presuppositions that become the loci of religious disagreement can go yet further. For the Jew, the Christian, and the Stoic all hold that there is a Being who rules the world: according to Jew and Christian, that Ruler acts in history, whereas according to the Stoic he does not. But there are other faiths that would deny the presupposition that (D) "The source of all being rules the world." The Neoplatonist, for example, denies this, as does the Hindu of the Advaita-Vedānta school, one of whose concepts was discussed in Chapter 8.

William Christian further points out that besides religious disagreements of the above-mentioned kind, in which different predicates are affirmed of the same subject (he calls these "doctrinal disagreements"), there are others in which different subjects are assigned to the same predicate; these latter he calls "basic religious disagreements." For example, the theist says that "God is the ground of being," but the pantheist says that "Nature is the ground of being." Other basic religious predicates attributed to different subjects in different religions are "the supreme goal of Life" (this is the Beatific Vision in Christianity; Nirvana in Buddhism); "that on which we unconditionally depend" (Allah in Islam; the God and Father of our Lord Jesus Christ in Christianity); "more important than anything else" (knowledge of one's true nature in Hinduism; worship of Jahweh in Judaism); "ultimate" (the Absolute, or Brahman, in Hinduism; Truth in humanism); "holy" (God in the theistic faiths; man in humanism). William Christian offers a complex and interesting theory of the relation between basic religious proposals and doctrinal proposals; but we are only concerned at the moment with his demonstration of how disagreements between religions may be located by uncovering the presuppositions of statements that might, at first sight, seem to have meaning only in the context of a particular religion, and thus not to be candidates for either agreement or disagreement on the part of other religions. We have seen that there are real disagreements concerning religious belief-proposals; that is to say, there are many belief-proposals that are accepted by the adherents of one religion but rejected by those of another.

So far, then, the problem posed at the beginning of this chapter has refused to be banished. There is however another approach to it which deserves to be considered.

CRITIQUE OF THE CONCEPT OF "A RELIGION"   In his important book *The Meaning and End of Religion*,[4] Wilfred Cantwell Smith challenges the familiar concept of "a religion," upon which much of the traditional problem of conflicting religious truth claims rests. He emphasizes that what we call a religion—an empirical entity that can be traced historically and mapped geographically—is a human phenomenon. Christianity, Hinduism, Judaism, Buddhism, Islam, and so on are human creations whose history is part of the wider history of human culture. Cantwell Smith traces the development of the concept of a religion as a clear and bounded historical phenomenon and shows that the notion, far from being universal and self-evident, is a distinctively Western invention which has been exported to the rest of the world. "It is," he says, summarizing the outcome of his detailed historical argument, "a surprisingly modern aberration for anyone to think that Christianity is true or that Islam is—since the Enlightenment, basically, when Europe began to postulate religions as intellectualistic systems, patterns of doctrine, so that they could for the first time be labeled 'Christianity' and 'Buddhism', and could be called true or false."[5] The names by which we know the various "religions" today were in fact (with the exception of "Islam") invented in the eighteenth century; and before they were imposed by the influence of the West upon the peoples of the world no one had thought of himself as belonging to one of a set of competing systems of belief concerning which it is possible to ask, "Which of these systems is the true one?" This notion of religions as mutually exclusive entities with their own characteristics and histories—although it now tends to operate as a habitual category of our thinking—may well be an example of the illicit reification, the turning of good adjectives into bad substantives, to which the Western mind is prone and against which contemporary philosophy has warned us. In this case a powerful but distorting conceptuality has helped to create phenomena answering to it, namely the religions of the world seeing themselves and each other as rival ideological communities.

Perhaps however, instead of thinking of religion as existing in mutually exclusive systems, we should see the religious life of mankind as a dynamic continuum within which certain major disturbances have from time to time set up new fields of force, of greater or lesser power, displaying com-

4 Wilfred Cantwell Smith, *The Meaning and End of Religion,* 1962 (New York: The New American Library Inc., Mentor Books, 1964).
5 Wilfred Cantwell Smith, *Questions of Religious Truth.* (London: Victor Gollancz Ltd., 1967), p. 73.

plex relationships of attraction and repulsion, absorption, resistance, and reinforcement. These major disturbances are the great creative religious moments of human history from which the distinguishable religious traditions have stemmed. Theologically, such moments are seen as intersections of divine grace, divine initiative, divine truth, with human faith, human response, human enlightenment. They have made their impact upon the stream of human life so as to affect the development of cultures; and what we call Christianity, Islam, Hinduism, Buddhism, are among the resulting historical-cultural phenomena. It is clear, for example, that Christianity has developed through a complex interaction between religious and non-religious factors. Christian ideas have been formed within the intellectual framework provided by Greek philosophy; the Christian church was moulded as an institution by the Roman Empire and its system of laws; the Catholic mind reflects something of the Latin Mediterranean temperament, whereas the Protestant mind reflects something of the northern Germanic temperament; and so on. It is not hard to appreciate the connections between historical Christianity and the continuing life of man in the western hemisphere; and of course the same is true in their own ways of all the other religions of the world.

This means that it is not appropriate to speak of a religion as being true or false, any more than it is to speak of a civilization as being true or false. For the religions, in the sense of distinguishable religiocultural streams within man's history, are expressions of the diversities of human types and temperaments and thought forms. The same differences between the Eastern and Western minds that are revealed in different conceptual and linguistic, social, political, and artistic forms, presumably also underlie the contrasts between Eastern and Western religion.

In *The Meaning and End of Religion* Cantwell Smith examines the development from the original religious event or idea—whether it be the insight of the Buddha, the life of Christ, or the career of Mohammed—to a religion in the sense of a vast living organism with its own credal backbone and its institutional skin. And he shows in each case that this development stands in a questionable relationship to that original event or idea. Religions as institutions, with the theological doctrines and the codes of behavior that form their boundaries, did not come about because the religious reality required this, but because such a development was historically inevitable in the days of undeveloped communication between the different cultural groups. But now that the world has become a communicational unity, we are moving into a new situation in which it becomes both possible and appropriate for religious thinking to transcend these cultural-historical boundaries. But what form might such new thinking take, and how would it affect the problem of conflicting truth claims?

TOWARD A POSSIBLE
SOLUTION

To see the historical inevitability of the plurality of religions in the past and its noninevitability in the future we must note the broad course that has been taken by the religious life of mankind. Man has been described as a naturally religious animal. He displays an innate tendency to experience his environment as religiously as well as naturally significant and to feel required to live in it as such. This tendency is universally expressed in the cultures of primitive man, with his belief in sacred objects, endowed with *mana,* and in a multitude of spirits needing to be carefully propitiated. The divine reality is here crudely apprehended as a plurality of quasi-animal forces. The next stage seems to have come with the coalescence of tribes into larger groups. The tribal gods were then ranked in hierarchies (some being lost by amalgamation in the process) dominated, in the Middle East, by great national gods such as the Sumerian Ishtar, Amon of Thebes, Jahweh of Israel, Marduk of Babylon, the Greek Zeus; and in India, by the Vedic high gods such as Dyaus (the sky god), Varuna (god of heaven), and Agni (the fire god). The world of such national and nature gods, often martial and cruel and sometimes requiring human sacrifices, reflected the state of man's awareness of the divine at the dawn of documentary history, some three thousand years ago.

So far, the whole development can be described as the growth of natural religion. That is to say, primitive spirit worship expressing man's fears of the unknown forces of nature, and later the worship of regional deities— depicting either aspects of nature (sun, sky, etc.) or the collective personality of a nation—represent the extent of man's religious life prior to any special intrusions of divine revelation or illumination.

But sometime after 1000 B.C. what has been called the golden age of religious creativity dawned. This consisted of a series of revelatory experiences occurring in different parts of the world, that deepened and purified man's conceptions of the divine, and that religious faith can only attribute to the pressure of the divine reality upon the human spirit. To quote A. C. Bouquet, "It is a commonplace with specialists in the history of religion that somewhere within the region of 800 B.C. there passed over the populations of this planet a stirring of the mind, which, while it left large tracts of humanity comparatively uninfluenced, produced in a number of different spots on the earth's surface prophetic individuals who created a series of new starting points for human living and thinking."[6] At the threshold of this period some of the great Hebrew prophets appeared (Elijah in the ninth century; Amos, Hosea, and the first Isaiah in the eighth century; and then Jeremiah in the seventh), declaring that they had heard the

---

[6] A. C. Bouquet, *Comparative Religion* (Harmondsworth, Middlesex: Penguin Books Ltd., 1941), pp. 77–78.

word of the Lord claiming their obedience and demanding a new level of righteousness and justice in the life of Israel. During the next five centuries, between about 800 and 300 B.C., the prophet Zoroaster appeared in Persia; Greece produced Pythagoras, and then Socrates and Plato, and Aristotle; in China Lao-tzu lived, and later Confucius; and in India this creative period saw the formation of the Upanishads and the lives of Gotama the Buddha, and Mahavira, founder of the Jain religion. Then, after a short gap, there came the writing of the *Bhagavad Gita* in India; and the life of Jesus of Nazareth and the emergence of Christianity; and after another gap, the prophet Mohammed and the rise of Islam.

It is important to observe the situation within which all these revelatory moments occurred. Communication between the different groups of humanity was then so limited that for all practical purposes men inhabited a series of different worlds. For the most part people living in China, in India, in Arabia, in Persia, were unaware of the others' existence. There was thus, inevitably, a multiplicity of local religions that were also local civilizations. Accordingly the great creative moment of revelation and illumination occurred separately within different cultures and influenced their development, giving them the coherence and confidence to expand into larger units, thus producing the vast religious-cultural entities that we now call world religions. So it is that in the past the different streams of religious experience and belief have flowed through different cultures, each forming and being formed by its own separate environment. There has of course been contact between different religions at certain points in history, and an influence—sometimes an important influence—of one upon another; but nevertheless, the broad picture is one of religions developing separately within their different historical and cultural settings.

In addition to noting these historical circumstances we need to make use of the important distinction between, on the one hand, man's encounters with the divine reality in the various forms of religious experience, and on the other hand, theological theories or doctrines that men have developed to conceptualize the meaning of these encounters. These two components of religion, although distinguishable, are not separable. It is as hard to say which came first as it is in the celebrated case of the hen and the egg. For they continually react upon one another in a joint process of development, experience providing the ground of our beliefs, but these in turn influencing the forms taken by our experience. And the different religions are different streams of religious experience, each having started at a different point within human history and each having formed its own conceptual self-consciousness within a different cultural milieu.

In the light of this it is possible to consider the hypothesis that the great religions are all, at their experiential roots, in contact with the same ultimate divine reality, but that their differing experiences of that reality, interacting over the centuries with the differing thought forms of differing cultures, have led to increasing differentiation and contrasting elaboration —so that Hinduism, for example, is a very different phenomenon from Christianity, and very different ways of experiencing and conceiving the divine occur within them. However now that in the "one world" of today the religious traditions are consciously interacting with each other in mutual observation and dialogue, it is possible that their future developments may move on gradually converging courses. For during the next centuries each group will presumably continue to change, and it may be that they will grow closer together, so that one day such names as "Christianity," "Buddhism," "Islam," "Hinduism," will no longer adequately describe the then current configurations of man's religious experience and belief. I am not thinking here of the extinction of human religiousness in a universal secularization. That is of course a possible future, and indeed many think it the most likely future to come about. But if man is an indelibly religious animal he will always, even amidst secularization, experience a sense of the transcendent by which he will be both troubled and uplifted. The future I am envisaging is accordingly one in which the presently existing religions will constitute the past history of different emphases and variations, which will then appear more like the different denominations of Christianity in North America or Europe today than like radically exclusive totalities.

If the nature of religion, and the history of religion, is indeed such that a development of this kind begins to take place in the remaining decades of the present century and during the succeeding twenty-first century, what would this imply concerning the problem of the conflicting truth claims of the different religions in their present forms?

We may distinguish three aspects of this question: differences in modes of experiencing the divine reality; differences of philosophical and theological theory concerning that reality, or concerning the implications of man's religious experience; and differences in the key or revelatory experiences that unify a stream of religious experience and thought.

The most prominent and important example of the first kind of difference is probably that between the experience of the divine as personal and as nonpersonal. In Judaism, Christianity, Islam, and the important strand of Hinduism which is focused by the *Bhagavad Gita,* the Ultimate is apprehended as personal goodness, will, and purpose under the different names of Jahweh, God, Allah, Krishna. On the other hand in Hinduism as interpreted by the Advaita Vedānta school, and in Thervada Buddhism, ultimate reality is apprehended as nonpersonal. Mahayana Buddhism seems to be in an intermediate state, with a tendency away from the latter toward the former point of view. Again, within the theistic faiths, there is the contrast between the experience of God as stern judge and as gracious friend, as Law Giver or as Father. There is, I think, in principle no difficulty in holding that these pairs can be understood as complementary rather than as incompatible. For if, as every profound form of theism has affirmed, God is infinite and therefore exceeds the scope of our finite human categories, he may be both personal Lord and nonpersonal Ground of Being; both judge and father, source alike of justice and of love. At any rate, there is a program for thought in the exploration of what Aurobindo called "the logic of the infinite"[7] and the question of the extent to which predicates that are incompatible when attributed to a finite reality may no longer be incompatible when referred to infinite reality.

The second type of difference is in philosophical and theological theory or doctrine. Such differences, and indeed conflicts, are not merely apparent; but they are part of the still developing history of human thought, and it may be that in time they will be transcended. For they belong to the historical, culturally conditioned aspect of religion, which is subject to change. When one considers, for example, the immense changes that have come about within Christian thought during the last hundred years, in response to the development of modern biblical scholarship and the modern physical and biological sciences, one can set no limit to the further developments that may take place in the future. A book of contemporary Christian theology (post-Darwin, post-Einstein, post-Freud), taking account of biblical source criticism and taking for granted a considerable demythologization of the New Testament world view, would have been quite unrecognizable as Christian theology two centuries ago. Comparable responses to modern science are yet to occur in many of the other religions of the world; but they must inevitably come, sooner or later. And when all the main religious traditions have been through their own encounter with modern science, they will probably have undergone as considerable an internal development as has Christianity. Besides, there will be an increasing influence of each faith upon every other as they meet and interact more and more freely within the "one world" of today. In the light of all this, the future that I have speculatively projected does not seem impossible.

However, it is the third kind of difference that constitutes the largest difficulty in the way of religious agreement. For each religion has its holy founder or scripture or both in which the divine reality has been revealed— the Vedas, the Torah, the Buddha, Christ and the Bible, the Koran. And wherever the Holy is revealed, it claims an absolute response of faith and worship, which thus seems incompatible with a like response to any other claimed disclosure of the Holy. Within Christianity, for example, this

[7] Sri Aurobindo. *The Life Divine* (Pondicherry: Sri Aurobindo Ashram, 1949), Book II, chap. 2.

absoluteness and exclusiveness of response has been strongly developed in the doctrine that Christ was uniquely divine, the only Son of God, of one substance with the Father, the only mediator between God and man. But this traditional doctrine, formed in an age of substantial ignorance of the wider religious life of mankind, gives rise today to an acute contradiction. For on the one hand, Christianity teaches that God is the Creator and Lord of all men and that he loves all men and seeks their final good and salvation; and on the other hand that only by responding in faith to God in Christ can men be saved. This means that infinite love has ordained that men can be saved only in a way that in fact excludes the majority of them; for the greater part of all the human beings who have been born since man began have lived either before Christ or outside the borders of Christendom. In an attempt to meet this glaring paradox, Christian theology has developed a doctrine according to which those outside the circle of Christian faith may nevertheless be saved. For example, the Second Vatican Council of the Roman Catholic Church, 1963–1965, declared that "Those who through no fault of theirs are still ignorant of the Gospel of Christ and of his Church yet sincerely seek God and, with the help of divine grace, strive to do his will as known to them through the voice of their conscience, those men can attain to eternal salvation."[8] This represents a real movement in response to a real problem;[9] but nevertheless it is only an epicycle of theory, complicating a basically dubious dogmatic system and not going to the heart of the problem. The epicycle is designed to cover theists ("those who sincerely seek God") who have had no contact with the Christian gospel. But what of the nontheistic Buddhists and nontheistic Hindus? And what of those Muslims, Jews, Buddhists, Hindus, Jains, Parsees, etc., both theists and nontheists, who have heard the Christian gospel but have preferred to adhere to the faith of their fathers?

Thus it seems that if the contradiction at the heart of the traditional Christian attitude to non-Christian faiths is to be resolved, Christian thinkers must give even more radical thought to the problem than they have as yet done. It is however not within the scope of this book to suggest a plan for the reconstruction of Christian or other religious doctrines.

[8] *Dogmatic Constitution on the Church,* Art. 16.
[9] The movement is developed by a group of Roman Catholic theologians in Joseph Neuner, ed., *Christian Revelation and World Religions* (London: Burns & Oates Ltd., 1967).

FOR FURTHER READING

NOTE: Numerous suggestions for further reading are contained in the footnotes to the various chapters of this book. The following are some more general works.

ABERNETHY, GEORGE L., and THOMAS A. LANGFORD, eds., *Philosophy of Religion: A Book of Readings,* 2nd. ed. New York: The Macmillan Company, 1968. A comprehensive volume of readings.

ALSTON, WILLIAM P., ed., *Religious Belief and Philosophical Thought.* New York: Harcourt Brace Jovanovich, Inc., 1963. Readings.

BURTT, E. A., *Types of Religious Philosophy,* rev. ed. New York: Harper & Row, Publishers, 1951. Provides an accurate account of the points of view of Roman Catholicism; conservative, liberal, and neo-orthodox Protestantism; humanism; ethical idealism; scientism; and agnosticism.

CHARLESWORTH, M. J., *Philosophy of Religion: The Historic Approaches.* London: Macmillan & Company Ltd.; New York: Herder and Herder, Inc., 1972. Valuable historical introduction.

DUCASSE, C. J., *A Philosophical Scrutiny of Religion.* New York: The Ronald Press Company, 1953. A very clearly written book, the title of which exactly describes its contents.

FLEW, ANTONY, and ALASDAIR MacINTYRE, eds., *New Essays in Philosophical Theology.* London: Student Christian Movement Press Ltd.; New York: The Macmillan Company, 1955. Contains a collection of some of the most interesting recent writings on the topic of the problems of religious language.

HICK, JOHN, ed., *Classical and Contemporary Readings in the Philosophy of Religion,* 2nd ed. Englewood Cliffs, N.J.: Prentice-Hall, Inc., 1970. A comprehensive volume of readings.

———, *The Existence of God* (Paperback). New York: The Macmillan Company, 1964. Contains a collection of the sources for a critical study of the theistic arguments.

MITCHELL, BASIL, ed., *The Philosophy of Religion.* (Oxford Readings in Philosophy). London: Oxford University Press, 1971. Important recent reprinted papers.

INDEX